"*Awake* is an invitation to let go of expectations for the life you think you should be living and instead abide with Christ, trusting that He really is writing the best story. Anjuli's appeal to wake up to the presence of God is a sweet reminder of truth for women of all ages."

Ruth Chou Simons, *Wall Street Journal* bestselling author, artist, and founder of gracelaced.com

"A breath of fresh air for the one who feels heavy, hopeless, or held up in a waiting room for something new to begin. In the pages of *Awake*, you will feel a new sense of hope and a gracious dose of courage. Vulnerable and brave, refreshing and real, Anjuli shares profound stories and insights that will help you stop waiting for your life to start and instead discover the full life in Jesus Christ that's available to you today."

Hosanna Wong, international speaker, spoken-word artist, and bestselling author of *How (Not) to Save the World*

"Anjuli is the gentle whisper in a loud world, reminding us that it's okay if we slow down, pause even, to wake up to the lives we're living. If you're afraid to get quiet with yourself and ask yourself the hard questions you've been avoiding with busyness, this is the book for you. Don't go the journey alone, don't let the guilt suck you in, don't let fear hold you back from discovering and uncovering not only who you are but who you are becoming. You have a purpose; let these pages remind you of what it is."

Jenna Kutcher, host of the *Goal Digger* podcast

"Anjuli, in a way that only she is gifted to do, has called us into a sacred space—once again—to lay aside false belief for truth. This is the reset message we need."

Kennesha N. Buycks, author and owner of Restoration House

"This book feels like getting to have a long conversation with a dear friend. Anjuli Paschall's honesty is a healing gift."

K.J. Ramsey, licensed professional counselor and author of *This Too Shall Last*

"In her book *Awake*, Anjuli Paschall invites us to embrace the divine within the mundane and often chaotic moments of our lives. I've always admired the way that Anjuli laces her words together to deliver piercing truths that soothe my weary soul. This book has awakened my heart to the beauty of God's tender presence in every moment of my life. Especially the moments that I'd rather sleep through."

Cassandra Speer, vice president of Her True Worth

"In a world that constantly urges us to do and be more, *Awake* feels like a long drink of cool water on a hot day. Anjuli's words bring refreshment because she isn't prescribing a list of things to wake up and do. Rather, she is reminding me to wake up to God and all the good He has in store for me. It's a message we need now more than ever."

Greta Eskridge, author of *Adventuring Together: How to Create Connections and Make Lasting Memories with Your Kids* and *100 Days of Adventure*

AWAKE

Books by Anjuli Paschall

Stay

Awake

AWAKE

*Paying Attention to What Matters Most
in a World That's Pulling You Apart*

ANJULI PASCHALL

BETHANYHOUSE
a division of Baker Publishing Group
Minneapolis, Minnesota

© 2022 by Anjuli Paschall

Published by Bethany House Publishers
11400 Hampshire Avenue South
Minneapolis, Minnesota 55438
www.bethanyhouse.com

Bethany House Publishers is a division of
Baker Publishing Group, Grand Rapids, Michigan

Printed in the United States of America

Library of Congress Cataloging-in-Publication Data
Names: Paschall, Anjuli, author.
Title: Awake : paying attention to what matters most in a world that's pulling you apart / Anjuli Paschall.
Description: Minneapolis, Minnesota : Bethany House Publishers, a division of Baker Publishing Group, [2022] | Includes bibliographical references.
Identifiers: LCCN 2021046295 | ISBN 9780764238529 (cloth) | ISBN 9781493435975 (ebook)
Subjects: LCSH: Christian women—Religious life. | Spirituality—Christianity. | Awareness—Religious aspects—Christianity.
Classification: LCC BV4527 .P383 2022 | DDC 248.8/43—dc23
LC record available at https://lccn.loc.gov/2021046295

Cover design by Ann Gjeldum
Cover photography by Jacob Bell

The author is represented by Alive Literary Agency.

Baker Publishing Group publications use paper produced from sustainable forestry practices and post-consumer waste whenever possible.

22 23 24 25 26 27 28   7 6 5 4 3 2 1

Mom
For every cup of tea shared
For every "God thing" lived
For every song you've ever sung
Thank you.

Awake, O sleeper,
  and arise from the dead,
and Christ will shine on you.

EPHESIANS 5:14

Contents

Introduction

The Whole Truth

've spent most of my life trying to figure out how to be human. I know I *am* human. I know I am a living, moving, breathing, full of angst, anger, and tangible hope—human. I've tried to figure out how my body works and how my mind processes information. I've tried to understand how the physical relates to the spiritual world. I've worked tirelessly at navigating relationships and figuring out how to simply—get along with others. Yet, after all these years my soul is battered with the same bewildering questions: Am I living my life to the fullest? Am I doing what matters most? Am I fully awake? Honestly, I hate questions like these.

There is no better way to feel like a failure than to start really examining my life. That's why I truly dread New Year's. All the resolutions and finding your word for the year makes me want to take a long nap. It's like I'm buried in piles of laundry and everyone else is talking about organizing the cans in the pantry by alphabetical order. I just can't keep up. I can't figure out the human thing. The longing to live a beautiful life is compelling. Yet, I instantly feel pressure and anxiety when I look at my actual life. Where I want to be and where I actually am are drastically different. When I look at my every day, I'm unamused by it all. I'm stumbling at best to live intentionally and without being daily irritated by dumb things like a slow drive-thru lane or someone ignoring my text. I get pulled and yanked by social causes and signing petitions. The rabbit hole of what to do, how to do it, and when to do it is as mind-bending as an underground subway system. I'm rapidly approaching midlife, and I still don't fully know how to do life *right* or *well*. I feel like something is missing. I call it carpe diem syndrome—the fear of not living life to the fullest.

I've spent most of my life on hold. Wait till college is done; then I can get married. Wait till I'm married; then I can travel. Wait to travel until I have money. Wait to buy a house until I have a stable job. Wait to have a career until my babies are grown. Wait for better friends to come, a better church to be planted, a better car to drive. Wait till the weekend to relax. Wait to do the things I've always imagined doing *until*. Wait a second, I'm sprinting through life with a million commitments wondering, *What do I even want to do anymore*? So much of life is—hurry up and wait for some other day. We hold on and hold on and hold on until we forget what we are even holding on to and for what. This hold-and-wait way of living is so dismal, exhausting, and tiring that at some point it is easier to sleep than stay awake to wonder, to a dream, or to a hope of something different.

I've been alive 14,511 days. The sun rises. The sun sets. Another day. Sometimes in small moments when the world is quiet and asleep, I contemplate what it is to be alive. Thousands of beautiful hours are tethered together by laughter and longing, hurt and sorrow, breath, and beat. Each second composing our incredible reality. I'm afraid of life. The mere possibility of my existence feels fragile and somewhat inconsequential. I've had a slow-growing itch I've been trying to reach for most of my life. It's an itch for something more. I've longed for that.

At each momentous occasion, I thought the itch would resolve. I backpacked through Europe, lived in Asia, tasted the finest of food, lived among the poor, and danced with the wealthy. I've built a business, married a handsome man, had enough kids to fill a minivan, and taken in stray cats. All of these scratched the itch but didn't resolve it. Each were good, but somehow not enough. The desire for more persisted. At some point, I typically Googled some version of the question "Where are the best cities in the world to live with kids?" and I got lost in a fantasy for a few hours. But, of course, those searches only aggravate me more. I so desperately wanted one of these experiences to satisfy me like spreading creamy icing onto a cake, but none of them did. I lie awake at night with this longing, the quiet itch for more.

I thought the desire for *more* meant that I was ungrateful or greedy. Maybe I just needed to be more content. But I couldn't deny my desire. It was there. I was hungry for more. I wanted more peace, more joy, more hope, more love, more of my soul-bursting-wide-open in glorious praise, more. I worked to get more. I chased hard after the illusive more. It had to be obtainable. If I just kept looking, pressing, ordering my priorities differently, getting a new system in place, planning a better trip, getting my kids to easier ages, the *more* I wanted would be found. But the more I sought after *more*, the further away it got from me. No matter how hard I tried, the dangling carrot could never be touched. The itch was always just out of reach—my carpe diem syndrome kicking into full gear.

I wanted to be awake and live life to the fullest, but I just couldn't figure out how to do it. I had spent so much time trying to appease my itch that I never stopped to understand it.

Looking, really looking, at my desire for this

I was hungry for more.

mysterious *more* meant I had to see myself, experience my lack, and face some of my demons. Sometimes it's easier to close my eyes and pretend than it is to see reality. When I was younger, I was afraid of sleeping alone, being left out, my mom dying, and spelling tests. Today, my fears range from public bathrooms and sick kids, to loved ones walking away from Jesus. I'm afraid of the IRS and when unknown numbers leave me voice messages. I'm always afraid of being caught, found out, or called out for something I did wrong or by mistake. But the older I get, the more I see one overarching fear in my life. I'm afraid I'll arrive at the end of my life, maybe it will be tomorrow or in fifty years, and realize that I never really lived. Looking at my itch meant my greatest fear was coming true. Even though I had so much, I was still unfulfilled. Gut punch. I was moving so fast trying to catch life that I was actually missing it. This terrified me. I was doing everything right, but something in me was wrong. And there remained the unreachable, pressure-mounting, shame-filled, untouchable—itch.

Do you know this itch too?

I've always interpreted the itch as though something was wrong. The itch was haunting me like a quiet echo inside my mind. It was my job to resolve it and get rid of it. People, social media, and every message on my screen said, "The way to true life is possible! With this course, a swipe up, or on sale today, you can get the life you've always wanted!" Maybe finding more meant giving away more of my time, resources, and money. Maybe I needed another cause to support, one more baby, or a chicken coop in a rural community. If the itch was going to find relief, it was up to me. So, I rolled up my soul-sleeves and I got to work punching that itch into submission. My goodness, it's exhausting fighting a shadow.

But what if the itch isn't mine to fix? What if there is more for me to follow?

What if that impossible place to scratch in the middle of my spine wasn't for me to reach with a long stick and Gumby arms twisted like a bendy straw always on the verge of snapping? What if the itch is a whispered invitation from God, *I have something more for you*? The itch is an invitation into a better story. Here, the adventure begins.

God is on a mission to move us into a life of abiding. The work of the Spirit right now is to transform my heart habits from living a life of autonomy (the self-laws I've made) to a life of with-ness with God. Living life to the fullest doesn't have anything to do with my ability to carpe diem, but everything to do with living a life of connectedness. Awake-ness is with-ness. It is a call to wake up to the story beneath the story.

I recently watched a movie with my husband, Sam. There were guns, fighting scenes, and an assassin trying to start a new life. When I turned to fall asleep, I was unsatisfied with the film. Yet, Sam pulled out all these deeper themes I didn't even notice. Apparently, the assassin was fighting her way to freedom by healing the broken relationships in her past. I turned my head. *Really?* How did I miss that? How did I miss the real meaning of the story? It was hidden, laced, and nuanced throughout the dialogue and PG-13 violence. The story wasn't about killing the bad guys. The story beneath the story was about redemption.

I think I miss the meaning of the story a lot. Not just in movies, but in my real life. I think my story is about what college to attend, career paths, vacations, buying a house, managing a nap schedule, or getting the backyard in order. I think my story is about motherhood, planning meals, community service, healthy relationships, a well-balanced diet, hospitality, staff meetings, or sneaking in a workout before the day is done. The strained relationship with my spouse, annoyance with an inefficient system, the fluctuating housing market, heartbreaking adoption process, leadership that is tone deaf is the story I might be struggling with at this moment, but it isn't the whole story. God is waking me up, through those stories, to the real story. So often we ask, *God, what do you want me to do?* rather than the more pertinent question, *God, what are you doing?* I can focus all of my time, attention, and energy on figuring out my life circumstances. I can spend countless hours trying to finagle my life into getting the maximum amount of comfort. These stories consume all my thoughts, affection, and attention. Those are the places where I start, but not where I am intended to end. I'm learning to follow these stories like signs leading me to the real story.

The real story is underneath all of these. So often I stop at the signs thinking I've arrived at my destination. How disappointing it would be if I stopped at the "10 miles to Big Sur" sign off Highway 1 and didn't continue up the curvy, steep, one-lane road to the top. If I stopped at the sign, I'd miss the expansive ocean view slowly opening my soul yet sewing it back together at the same time. As I approach the middle of my life, I think I've stopped at the arrows and not followed to where they intended to lead me. I have marriage, kids, friends, career, church, yet I have that persistent itch like something is missing.

Here, right here, is where God's whisper comes: *I have something more for you.* My itch is a gift into a good journey. I want *that* adventure. I want the story beneath the story. Then I began to see it. It is there. Hidden, tucked, and woven beneath all the other stories. It's a journey into connectedness. It's an unwrapping of the greatest gift. An awakening to discover how the actual real-life presence of God in my life changes everything. The story beneath the story. It is always the same. Underneath my daily irritations, the rapid news cycle, family drama, and mail mounting up, the story beneath these stories is always one and the same—God is waking me up to himself. My average existence folds into God's massive love for the world and intimate love for me. I belong here. Here is the more I've been craving.

I want to be awake to the real story. I want to live my life present to what God is doing and not just focused on what I'm supposed to do. So many stories are vying for my attention. So many voices demand my eye contact. I am pulled wide and thin, and I'm tied to my phone, trying to manage the noise. If I'm not careful I'll live a story that doesn't belong to me or become fixated on a daydream of something better than being right here. I refuse to chase a mirage that promises water but leaves me parched. I want to lean into the story that matters most. I want to stay awake to God's presence with me. I don't want to blink. I don't want to miss a meaningful, wide-awake life.

I want all of this, but how?

Follow the itch.

Our souls pry apart slowly, yet at times, they pop open like a spring. In a moment, by the smell of almond trees or the hum of a distant train, we can be transported to a place inside ourselves we've long lost contact with. We have windows to our bodies. Our senses allow direct access to our deepest places. They are the backstage passes to our becoming. Through taste, touch, sight, smell, sound, memory we can become awake to God's presence of love in our lives. He meets our souls through the quiet ding of the dishwasher, the expansive valley parting the way through mountain ranges, and the frothy foam ceiling on our morning coffee greeting us into a new day. With our eyes we read psalms, hymns, and spiritual songs. Our souls awaken.

In the scraping of wipers scratching frost off windshields and soft ice in sweet lemonade, God greets us gently with kindness. With butter slathered over slices of fresh sourdough bread, fried eggs cackling like the sound of schoolgirls giggling, and sunlight bursting into sleepy kitchens like a laser show, God is waking us up to His constant presence. In response, we stay soft, open, and on the lookout for His invitations.

Our senses and everyday stories become like signs leading us to the story beneath the story. When our everyday stories of frustration, hope, beauty, and apathy connect with God's love pursuit story, there is the more (joy, hope, peace, and faith) we've been desiring. The layers are peeled back. We can begin to see what's really going on. We can see the real story. Through the compelling act of paying attention, we start to discover the story beneath the story of God in our lives. It's wild and safe and everything we've ever wanted.

Sister, take a moment to look back on your life. When were you the most awake? Really, think about it. Your mind may stream through a series of significant events: graduations, your wedding day, your first kiss, a thesis paper you worked hard on, a coveted promotion. All of these were good, but they slowly slip out of your mind. To your surprise, you recall a two-a.m. conversation you had with a friend when you were in college. You shared things you'd never shared before. You were connected closely to another person, and something in you woke up. You remember that time when God used your unique gifts for the good of others and a burning light turned on inside of you. You were connected to your calling. Your memory takes you back to a lonely night when in the most unexpected moment, you saw a shooting star. Somehow you knew the streamer of light dazzling like a sparkler across the cave-dark sky was meant for you. You were connected to creation. But, most certainly, you could never forget the exact second when Jesus saved you. When you were flat on your face, God loved you. You were connected to your creator. These intersections of awake-ness weren't milestones, accomplishments, or something you coerced; they were about connection. Mysteriously, instead of achieving awake-ness, you were actually receiving it.

Sister, highlight this: if you want a rich life without regret, it will never come from chasing after it. Waking up has nothing to do with your ability to make it happen, hustle, or push harder. Living life to the fullest isn't something we do with more book clubs, wine nights, weekend getaways, or the next home project. It isn't found when we sacrifice more, live with less, or give away all we have. It won't come when you plant a garden, have a happy family, reach your ideal weight, or make enough money. Look at the times in your life when you have been most awake and let those be your guide into the future. If you want to truly be awake, it comes through meaningful connection to others, connection to your calling, connection to your voice, connection to creation, and connection to your creator. Connection, connection, connection. Follow your itch into the story beneath the story. God is inviting you into more and more soul-awakening connection.

> If you want a rich life without regret, it will never come from chasing after it.

I won't prescribe a list of how-to's or tell you to just do it like I do. I won't make court-like arguments or graph unreachable goals. I will, however, promise you this—the life you want is possible, and you don't have to lose your soul trying to get it. I'm not referring to financial stability, your kids turning out okay, or the easy life you want. I am referring to a life you *really* want. The life that lives below all the other things. I know what you want because it is what every human wants. We want true, meaningful, rich, soul-satisfying connection. We want to be known intimately, understood without justification, and loved unconditionally.

Sister, this is possible. I know you have voices that tell you otherwise, but I stand convinced it is true. I've lived it. I've tasted, touched, and felt it. Without waking up to God's presence with you, you will meander through your days sleepwalking. You will continuously feel stuck, lost, disconnected, and adrift. You will have low-grade anxiety, frantic thoughts, numbing strategies to get through the day, and pills to get you through the night. You will be with people you've known for years but feel sadly unknown. Life will feel like a bland dish; you'll eat it, but it won't be savored. If you are honest with yourself, you will hear a nagging, haunting, and confusing desire for *more*. There is another way. Wake up—God is inviting you on a new adventure.

Sister, I'm inviting you to live at the edge of the abyss. Stand at the unknown places of your soul and story. This adventure doesn't have an itinerary or departure times. It is an inward journey. The journey might have long stretches of dry desert, steep terrain, and slippery rocks. Winter storms and blazing heat will meet you on the road ahead. This adventure will only require one thing of you—a willing heart. But I promise it is worth it. At times, it will be almost too easy. You will sit and reflect and feel nothing but gratitude. Other times, you will be tempted to fall back asleep because the road will narrow, and shadows will grow scary. But stay awake. In the hidden places of your heart, you won't be alone; you'll find connection with your friend Jesus.

Pay attention. God does the waking and prodding. He leads the way. Jesus is the compass, map, and true north. God waking you up to the story beneath your story can be as abrupt as a rooster crowing before daybreak, invasive and intruding. Sometimes it can be subtle, quiet, and as silent as bubbles floating by. Other times God's soul nudge can be so obvious we cover our mouths in sheer amazement and silent tears. Nonetheless, the love of God is persistent to penetrate even the coldest corners of our hearts. Consider this book as a gong, a gentle song, or a dinner bell calling you to wake up to certain parts of your story. God is here. God is present. God is pursuing us in second-by-second love. Like calling a child awake, God nudges, repeats, and carries us up and out of bed. God pulls wide the shades and invites us to see the sunrise. A relationship with God is *being* with Christ no matter how horrible or happy the adventure may be. Watch the show, hang the clothes, have the hard conversation, drink another cup of tea, be with Jesus. True awake-ness isn't about what we do, but who we are connected to. Your itch for more soothed.

I want to wake up to beauty, delight, and everything that is holy in our world. I don't want to shut off my joy because I was too scared to see my pain. I don't want to nervously navigate my life one to-do list, text, and espresso shot at a time. I want to engage in my one exquisite life, task by task, boring or not, excruciating or not, anxiety-filled or not, awake to the wonder of God's presence with me. I want real connection. I want God more than I want anything else. Or it would be more honest to say—I *want* to want God more than anything else.

Tomorrow is day 14,512. I'll most likely live it out with some sort of fear. I'll check my phone for security before I check in with Jesus. I'll worry about everything that I have to do or haven't done. I'll nervously putter, trying to get people's approval. God isn't concerned with results, quick changes, and "just get it right." He is always making room for my heart to rest in His. God is always joyfully tapping on the window

> God is always making room for my heart to rest in His.

of my body. It brings Him delight to wake up my soul to His love. It is a never-ending surprise party just for me or like the instant giddiness of finding a forgotten twenty-dollar bill in my back pocket. I hear love in the low, sturdy sound of cello strings, see it in a cinematic moonrise calling me to sleep, taste it in the salty crackers my kids didn't finish at lunch, and feel it in the softness of my favorite worn-in sweatshirt reminding me the best things get softer with time. My irritations rise with the demands required of me, and I'm drawn back to my need for true rescue. I let myself dream without a straitjacket, and I watch where my heart goes when I'm not afraid. God's love tap is always inviting me to the story beneath the story.

This is the whole truth: no one knows how to be human. Even the most intelligent, witty, and all-put-together people are winging it at best. We are all stumbling through a darkened wood with just a match, a dying phone battery, a hope, and a cheap survival kit strapped to our backs. It's okay, though. It's okay because Jesus goes before us on this journey. God who grew limbs, lungs, and love all the way down to earth to be human with us. He teaches us how to be human. We don't have to figure it all out alone. I don't have to do everything. I just have control over one thing every single day of my God-given, beauty-orchestrated, grace-saturated, love-abounding, holy, and hand-picked life. It isn't complicated or confusing. It isn't overwhelming or even hard. I can open my eyes. That's it. I can wake up to God's love story.

My first book, *Stay*, invited you to simply be where you are. *Awake* asks the most pertinent follow-up question: "Now, where is God as you stay?" As you name where your heart really is, stay and be awake to the presence of God. This book is how I stumbled and discovered God's love story beneath my story. Stories about how I grew into my humanness marked with qualities, flaws, and grace-filled do-overs. It's how I stood at the edge of my abyss and instead of being afraid, to my surprise, I became awake. Take courage, sister. No more delays. No more putting life on hold. The time is now. Adventure rises with the sun. God is calling, whispering, wildly waving, "Wake up, wake up, wake up!"

1

My Name

Wake up to more meaning

My name is Anjuli. I've always had a love-hate relationship with my name. I love how it looks pretty on paper. I think a "j" in any name is elegant. It is so graceful and, in my opinion, a "j" in cursive is the jewel of all the letters. It's so quaint, humble, and yet, confident. My name is unique and interesting. But I also hate it. The pronunciation is tricky. At several turning points in my life, I've tried to change my name. In college, I introduced myself as "July" and at my MOPS group table, "Jules." At Starbucks or with any reservation I make, I don't even bother with all the back and forth and give my husband's name, "Sam." Close friends and family pronounce my name "Anjelie." New friends might say "Ann-Julie." When I meet someone for the first time, there is always a hint of awkward hesitation because, to be honest, I don't really know how to pronounce my name. People usually repeat my name back to me with a kind but questioning eye. My response is always the same: "Yes, that's how you say it." I smile and move on.

I was named after a book my mom read while her best friend, Juile, was dying of breast cancer. The book is *The Far Pavilions*, and the main character is a young Indian girl named Anjuli. I didn't know what my name actually meant while I was growing up, but I would learn soon enough. In the most unimaginable way and from the most unsuspecting person, I'd learn what the name *Anjuli* means. In my early twenties when my life felt meaningless, a doctor delivering me devastating news would surprise me with the meaning of my name.

My twenties were transformative years. I went through bouts of desolation, the always regrettable decision to cut bangs, and a newfound love for adult beverages. I experienced a lot of silence from God, who had always been so active, safe, and good before. I had mysterious health issues, ended a significant relationship, lost friendships, and moved back in with my parents (every college graduate's dream). What was the meaning of my life? Not just my life, but life at all.

A sacred tear began. A tearing of skin between my internal world and external world. I couldn't control the feelings I had been stuffing for so long. I was leaking. For me, leaking looked like locking myself in my room, listening to moody music, lighting candles, and being mad at my mom because she asked too many questions. With a hammer and nails, I hung a queen-sized yellow sheet to my bedroom wall. It draped long and hit the floor. With acrylic colors and the Cardigans playing, I painted my heart on the sheet. In bold black letters, I scribbled *Invisible*. I pinned magazine clippings and old photographs to my massive wall collage. It was a mosaic of words and stories and short phrases that were welling up inside of me. It was all my brokenness exposed on a bed linen. It was my pain. When I had to go to work or school, I'd take the sheet down from the wall, fold it up, and tuck it back under my bed. Hidden. I put my heart away. I did this every day.

If I'm honest, I've been putting my heart away all my life. It wasn't like I tried to hide. I just did. It was my habit and rhythm and way of life. I didn't know how to be vulnerable or myself. I was good at stuffing my heart into small places. I was always afraid, and for the first time I was waking up to feelings, thoughts, and fears I had never had before. My heart felt weak, fragile, and embarrassing. To feel safe and secure I'd borrow strength from other people. I'd borrow it from friends, leaders, sisters, or anyone who looked like they had the human thing figured out. I survived by following, learning, and keeping my real self out of sight.

> I've been putting my heart away all my life.

Most of my life, I've taken strength from my earliest friend, Krissa. She is candid and loyal and speaks her mind. She is sarcastic and blunt and strong. She doesn't care what people think about her. If I ever find myself in a situation where I don't know what to do, I recite these four letters to myself: "WWKD." What would Krissa do? I examine my situation through Krissa's eyes, and somehow, I feel more confident. If I'm in a social situation that feels daunting, those four letters pop into my head. I quietly chant to myself, "Be more like Krissa." The words give me the courage to make hard decisions.

I've found confidence from women spiritual leaders. When I had my first speaking engagement, I was terrified. Because I am a pastor's wife, there is an unspoken expectation to speak publicly (as well as love children's ministry, know everyone's name, and be at every event with a smile to name a few others). Though I don't mind being up front with a microphone, I don't love it either. The morning of the church's Christmas brunch I folded my message, printed out on computer paper, in half. I grabbed the book *Cold Tangerines* by one of my favorite writers at the time, Shauna Niequist, from the shelf. I tucked my words into hers. From the stage, I opened her book and read my message. I held her courage in my hands, and somehow she gave me strength to speak. Her strength transferred to me.

My sister Wanida is another person who is solid inside. She is two years older than I am. I've basically followed in her footsteps my entire life. She did show choir, so I did it. She studied abroad, so I did it. She shopped at Abercrombie and Fitch and cut her hair pixie short, so obviously, I did too. I'll never forget when I was pulling out my heart from under the bed every day and I decided to let her see me. I let her into my locked room, and she sat on my bed. I read to her out of my journal with tears and tissue and lots of over apologizing. Wanida, the one I always leaned on for strength, wasn't startled or bothered by what I shared. She let me read and cry and go on and on without interrupting. She didn't try to fix me or give me advice. When I was done reading her my secrets from out of my spiral red notebook, she said, "I believe in you." She believed I could do the brave work of becoming real. Wanida gave me courage that day. I had been borrowing it from her for so long. She breathed courage into my soul.

We all need soul breathers. We need people who are patient and kind and aren't surprised when secrets come out. We need people who won't be shocked when they see the truth or be afraid to hold our pain. We need people who offer grace and freedom and thoughtful questions. I'm not sure if I would have ever had the courage to keep going if it weren't for that moment sitting on my bed with my sister. So I did the next scary thing. I followed my fear. I became a fear chaser. Because when someone believes in you, anything feels possible. I pulled out my yellow sheet I had methodically hidden away every day. I secured the two corners up high and let the rest unfold to the ground like a scroll. It was as though the skin on the front side of my body was coming down to the floor too. I unlocked the door and let my heart hang wide open on the wall.

It was one moment of courage that led to the next. I let the door stay open. I became less and less afraid of who might walk by or what someone might think about the words *alone*, *afraid*, *guilty*, *ugly* I had painted in bold black lettering. When my courage was weak, I borrowed it from others. I needed their confidence to help buoy me through. I wish I was naturally confident like Krissa and Wanida and even Shauna (my best friend who doesn't know I exist). But I've always felt nervous on the inside. I've always looked for affirmation from others to feel safe. Even when my courage grows, I still don't feel entirely sturdy, so I keep borrowing courage from others when I need it.

I wrap the courage of others around me like a cape. I think about the cape that Joseph's father, Jacob, wrapped around him. The robe was sewn with spectacular colors. It inflamed envy, the scariest shade of green, in his brothers. I think about the cloak that the father flung over the shoulders of his prodigal son, who made unforgivable mistakes. He was now draped in holy forgiveness. I think about the baby wrapped in swaddling clothes. God became small and was kept warm in a cloth. Jesus used a cloth to wash the feet of His beloved friends and the ones He knew would betray and deny Him. On the dirt floor He bent low, cleaned filthy feet, and dried them with a towel. Strips of cloth wrapped Christ in the tomb. The hope of life was without a heartbeat and bound up in blood-drenched linen.

I don't just want to take on others' courage, I want my own. I want courage that doesn't disappear as quickly as a mean comment on a social media post appears. I need a pill so strong its effects won't wear off. I'm not sure how to get through this life without courage. I need courage to not lose myself, speak my mind, and walk the long, hard road with people I love. I need something stronger than a cape to protect me when all the lights go out, when people get sick, when I can't withstand one more punch of rejection. I think courage is less about bolstering up strength or right thinking or a radical change. For Jesus, courage wasn't mounting an attack, getting bigger, standing taller on a soap box. Courage wasn't pumping himself up or rousing a crowd with His charisma. Courage wasn't that He died, but that He walked into death even though there was terror in His heart. He accepted His cup of suffering. He kept walking toward the cross even though He could have run or won the war.

I needed this kind of face-any-kind-of-fear courage as I walked into the doctor's office the day I discovered the meaning of my name. I didn't want to go to the doctor's office. In fact, I'd ignored symptoms and avoided scheduling an appointment with the specialist for as long as I could. I remember walking into the cold building past the trees as barren as my soul. Late fall in San Diego dusts everything with a light frost. I sat awkwardly on the table. The white sheet they made me wear felt sun-dried and stiff. I was nearly naked under it, but sometimes the weight we carry inside of us is heavier than any weight on the outside. The crinkly tissue under me kept sticking to my bare skin. This felt impossible. It was awkward. I was alone. Trying to convince the doctor I was confident and mature enough to be there without a chaperone, I pulled my shoulders back and looked him directly in the eyes. The doctor held up the MRI results like he was mentally doing a math problem. The tumor in my brain was still there.

A tumor the size of a blueberry sat suctioned onto my pituitary gland. It wasn't dangerous enough to do surgery but was still big enough to cause problems. Cancerous—thank goodness, no. Problematic—most definitely. Terrifying— yes. It wasn't growing or shrinking, but it was exactly where it shouldn't be. He gently talked me through the next steps. It would mean medication for a lifetime, more appointments, and the possibility of never having children. He was kind and spoke softly with his Indian accent. He looked directly at me with "Do you understand?" eyes. He scribbled a prescription. Before he handed it to me, he paused. He said, "Anjuli," and looked up. "Do you know what your name means?" His question caught me off guard. I shook my head. I didn't tell the nice doctor that not only did I not know the meaning of my name, but I didn't know how to pronounce it either. He smiled. "Anjuli means the fragrance released from a love offering." I left the cold room not feeling cold. I left with the answers I didn't want, but more awake than I had ever been. Meaning changes everything.

I think in my search for the universal meaning of life, I forgot my meaning. This happens though, doesn't it? We run and push and pull. We hurry, chase, and fix. Then at some point we stop and wonder, *What is the point of all of this?* What's the point of *me*? Why do we frantically manage people's expectations, sign up for everything, or need the towels folded a certain way? Why do we worry about what the neighbors think, hold on to a grudge from decades ago, or carefully craft a comeback? We go and go and go, blindly forgetting where we are actually trying to get to. This was me. All the while, I was wondering why I was lacking so much courage.

Courage isn't a virtue that is a manifestation of itself. One doesn't go to war, fight, and die because of courage alone. No, someone dies on the battlefield or in the arena because a compelling reason drives them—freedom. Meaning drives the action. Meaning first, courage second. Meaning is what I am made of, my substance, and what defines me. If I didn't know my meaning, I would never have courage. If I don't know why on earth I'm alive at all, I'll never catch my balance. I'll always feel like I'm toppling over. On the day I left the doctor's office, I knew my meaning. Maybe I had always known it, but I had forgotten. The heaviness of my vices, the breaking down of my beliefs, the persistent pull of other voices, and the hurry-angst of life left me grappling instead of grounded.

My fear and my heart-sheet hanging on my bedroom wall, the courage I just couldn't get a grip on started to make sense. My soul felt centered. I could face the day with my tumor and my fear and my always shaky soul because God was giving me meaning. Even when I couldn't make sense of everything, I could keep walking forward with Christ because life had meaning.

> If I didn't know my meaning, I would never have courage.

The general meaning of my life—like everyone's—is to love and be loved by God with my entire heart, soul, mind, and strength. I am called to love God with all of me. In all things, God's glory is the goal. God goes before me and behind me. Much of the courage I will ever need in my small, sacred, beautiful life is this—God is with me. When my insides are weak and my heart-sheet on the wall is exposed, I am not alone. I can walk forward in life with terror in my soul because Jesus is with me. He is with me today as I pour the cereal and wait for the water to boil. He is with me as I wait for the email to come and as I wrangle my internal dialogues. When I walk with God, pay attention to His presence, adhere to His ways, I am loving Him.

But there is also a personal meaning for my life. Yes, one that is just for me. I know the meaning of my one and only life when I reflect on how God rescued me. My story is defined by the ways God freed me from legalism, harmful relationships, and a long season of sadness. My story mounts on moments when I knew I was made to care for hurting souls, buoy the spiritually broken, and guide others back to the love of God. When I walk in step with God's story of meaning in me, my life releases a rich aroma. I can feel it. Others can almost smell it. When I stay connected to who God has made me to be, I am awake.

> When I stay connected to who God has made me to be, I am awake.

I know your life is moving fast. Several hard relationships yank on you. Dozens of complicated thoughts nag on you. Your fears, trauma, and shame linger in you like an endless hangover. You wake up and go, go, go. The pressure to keep going is unrelenting. You don't have time, space, or energy to deal with anything that really needs to be dealt with, and getting dinner done on time is the best you can manage. I get it. Me too. But sometimes we must pause and ask ourselves, *What's the meaning of it?* We have to go back to the original Greek, the starting line, and the drawing board. For me, I had to hammer a yellow sheet to my bedroom wall. We have to ask ourselves, *What's the point of my life?*

We must know our *why*. We must know for certain why we do what we do. If you want to know your unique meaning in this big world, you'll find it at the intersection of your pain and

God's rescue. When we reflect on our story and the suffering we've overcome, we will start to see our meaning clearly. God always gives us meaning. He gives us our names. He changed Abram to Abraham, Sarai to Sarah, Jacob to Israel, Simon to Peter. Our names matter. They define us. Our truest definition comes out of the healing from our deepest pain. What happens when we have nothing determines everything for us, just like it did for Abraham, Sarah, and Peter, whose names changed at the most crucial point in their lives. God meets us right in the crevice of our greatest wounds and wakes us up to His presence. He doesn't just meet us there but transforms us there.

God gives us all new names (Revelation 2:17). Our new names identify our past and give us meaning to move forward. For example, if you overcame addiction, your new name might be—the one God set free. If you were abandoned, physically or emotionally, by a parent—the one God remembers. If you spent your whole life unseen and God finds you—the one God pursues. If you survived a devastating divorce—the one God eagerly wants. If God made a way for you out of an impossible situation—the one God finds worthy. If God used your average abilities, looks, and limited education to help others—the one God adores. If God brought you out of darkness—the one God shines His light on.

Maybe you need to remember your unique meaning in this big world. You need to know why you exist in the first place. If you're like me, you need the reminder like notifications flashing, popping up on your phone. They interrupt life but also keep us connected to it. So often we see interruptions as a bad thing.

They seem like a detour from the thing we want. But what if interruptions are wake-up calls? What if they are calling you to come back to your *why* and the way God defines you?

In the Gospel of John, the author repeatedly refers to himself as *the disciple whom Christ loved*. For years, I read this and was completely bothered by it. John's audacity to say *he* was the one that Christ loved seemed so arrogant. But I think I was wrong. I think John discovered his purpose, his pulse, his identity, and the significant meaning of his life. He said it over and over as a reminder to himself and others of this radical truth. John walked into every room, every relationship, every conflict, and every celebration attentive to his meaning. John—the one Christ loved.

What if we took our meaning into our everyday world with us? Our general meaning is to love and be loved by God. Our personal meaning to be a vessel of God's love to others in a unique way based on our stories. If our souls were suctioned to the meaning God has given us, we would have all the courage we need to face impossible situations. In our quiet moments, fearful ones, dull ones, let our meaning be ever present. Let it be what defines us when we wake up, what inspires us as we walk the long day of arduous tasks, and what determines how we welcome others. Everywhere we go and no matter what we do, we repeat it like John did because it is the most important and beautiful thing about us.

Meaning is fundamental. Meaning matters. It is your lane. Stay centered. Stay right there. A million voices will scream, demand, and insist you need to do more or do things differently, but don't budge. Don't shy away from the path God has put you on. Be undeterred by what culture, prominent people, or your critics think about you. Through motherhood, marriage, and the relationships Jesus brings to you, stay awake to your meaning. Through your service, career changes, and life choices, remember who called you by name and don't be afraid. If you want to really be awake, stay close to your redemption story. Remember your places of pain and the times you survived when you almost wished for death. Remember the ways God answered prayers you barely even prayed, just silently hoped for. Remember the ways God walked with you. Now, watch courage rise. You don't have to fight for it, cling to it, or tattoo it to your skin. You just get to receive it. What glory our lives bring God when we live like this. What a fragrance we are.

Wake up, sister. I know it is scary to wake up to fears, feelings, and the thoughts you've kept quiet. I know it's terrifying to be real. I know you tell yourself to put your desires back to sleep. For a moment, relax your fingers, tilt your head right and left, unclench your jaw. You are real and your fears keep your body so tied up.

If you haven't found your meaning, look for it. It's fundamental. Without meaning, you are just spinning circles around courage and not living through it. You are trying to put out your fires with kerosene. You are treading water in the shallow end when you could just stand up. You are looking everywhere for the source of courage, except the one place it is found. You don't have to borrow courage from others anymore. As you step into the meaning of your life, courage will come.

Stop tucking your heart away. The hushed corners of your soul are allowed to speak. Your life has meaning. In wet cement on the foundation of your life, let God write out what your unique meaning is. I stand on these words when life feels scary: *safe, daughter, seen, held, liked, loved,* and *the one God could never lose.* When I stay here, with Christ, my courage is activated.

The words scripted on my sheet began to give me power instead of stealing it. Through being seen, my life was becoming an offering. Through my loneliness, guilt, and fear, God didn't back away, but was awakening me to love. Through my sadness and the sickness that was in my brain and the brokenness in my soul, my meaning was being made known. I was growing stronger, even though I felt depleted. The story beneath my health issues, my lack of direction, and my fear of seeing myself and being seen was that God was drawing me closer to the meaning of my specific life. He saw all of me and liked me anyway. In and through all these things, I was received as a fragrance.

I imagine how smells dwell and occupy space. I think about the delicate lavender scent lingering on my kitchen shelf right now, reminding me of summers past. I think about how smells layer together like stew simmering for hours, intoxicating my senses with comfort. When I walk into my favorite brick-and-mortar shop, tropical fruits and sweet citrus scents instantly enamor my soul like a familiar song. I never want to leave. Lemongrass, chopped and submerged into my dad's Thai curry, sends up swirls of sour and spice like streamers inviting me to a party. Smells envelop me.

My friend Ashley always smells like sweet peaches. With every hug, my heart is held by love. Her fragrance isn't only from her perfume; it radiates out from who she is—kind, generous, and warm. I think we all know people in our lives who radiate love like this. Beauty, gratitude, and joy flow almost effortlessly out of them. Their circumstances could be dire, yet they have an internal light. We don't just see it, but we sense it. We smell it. We want to be around it. I want to be this kind of person. The kind who glows on the inside and outside. When people are in my presence, I want them to sense love. The scent of Christ. This is what my name means.

The doctor that day thought he was delivering bad news, but he didn't. He wrote me a new prescription for life. I knew if I were to get sick, I wouldn't suffer alone. I knew I didn't need to siphon strength from friends, sisters, and coworkers for the rest of my life. I didn't need to lean on my knowledge, abilities, or inner confidence for courage. Instead, I leaned more into the story Jesus was writing in me. As I leaned, I let Christ come closer. As I know my purpose, every doubt inside of me settles. I feel unstoppable.

I wasn't afraid to let the inside of me live on the outside anymore. The yellow sheet hung proudly on my wall until I didn't even notice it anymore. A few months later, I would even display my soul sheet in an art show for strangers to see. My heart lived on the outside of my chest the way I think hearts are supposed to live—breathing, beautiful, and exposed.

I was awake now to my meaning. His meaning in me. You can call me Anjelli, Ann-Julie, or July. I don't care how you say it. What matters is that my name means something. I mean something. In all that I am, in all that I do, in everything that I face in life, God receives my life as an offering of love. He sustains me. My soul is held suspended and secure. I become full. My name is Anjuli, and to God, my life is a fragrance.

2

RSVP

Wake up to more acceptance

sat across from the boy I liked. Sam was the one. The boy I
had given my whole, gushy, young, fully-beating heart to.
Occasionally, we studied at Barnes and Noble, but in truth,
we went there because we always wanted to be together. Every
morning, afternoon, night, we wanted to be within reach. Yet,
this night felt different. I had a hard time making eye contact
with him. The space between us felt thick instead of free. My
skin was like a strong shield, impenetrable. It was uncomfortable because I didn't know how to evade his intense eye contact.
Sometimes the absence of connection says more than any words
ever could. I tried to speak, but my words felt vacant, robotic,
and monotone. Words not held by feelings fall flat. Yet, Sam
never flinched or looked away once. His eyes pierced me like

a spotlight on a prisoner trying to escape. With kindness, he spoke. "I can't be with you if you don't let me in. If I don't know you, all of you, I can't love you." He never would have said it was an ultimatum, but I knew it was. If I didn't let Sam past my skin-shield, then he couldn't be with me. He didn't want to just know my stories, he wanted to know my secrets.

I couldn't sleep that night. I had never let anyone all the way in before, into the deep, dark places. The places even I am too terrified to look at. The place where the silenced stories, half lies, and unwanted photos live. I have a cave of quiet inside of me. It's damp in there. It's abandoned, scary, and unexplored. A few people knew some of my secrets, but no one knew all of them. My master bedroom friends (my closest ones) knew a lot, but even they didn't know all the details. I'm so afraid of rejection. If someone saw all my ugliness and then walked away, I'm not sure I'd ever be able to get out of bed again.

No one in my life has seen me with true clarity. No human has held all of me. I can be transparent, but vulnerability is different. Transparency is when I reveal the information from the outside looking in. Vulnerability is when I expose myself from the inside out. It's when I let people actually see me—my feelings, fears, and frantic rawness. Vulnerability makes my soul flutter like a bird with a broken wing. Vulnerability makes me feel just that—broken. Keeping people on the periphery is no accident. I keep people close, but not too close. I want connection, but I'm afraid to be seen. Really seen. I surround my innermost world with walls. I'm on the inside; everyone else can stay safely on the outside thank.you.very.much.

I test people who attempt to get too close. I am constantly testing. If someone is trying to climb my walls, I put out traps. If someone dares to come close, I'll be sure they pay the price. My traps are tricky. If a friend wants to scale my walls, they must pass my series of small tests or they get sent to the back of the line. For instance, if I share the smallest piece of information about my life and a week or two later, they don't mention it again, then like a canon, they get shot out of my inner space. If someone checks their phone when I'm telling them something personal, then the wall gets thicker. If I don't get an email response in a timely manner, then it just confirms what I already believed: they don't really care about me anyway. I reject them before they have a chance to hurt me anymore. The barricade grows higher. If people want in, they have to pass my series of impossible tests. But I make the rules. I hold all the cards. I'm the only one who knows the instructions. To this point, everyone had failed. It only proved my deepest, darkest, most lonely cave-living belief—no one likes me. I look around; the evidence is damning. No one passes.

After the night at Barnes and Noble when he gave me the ultimatum, we went on a road trip to Arizona to see Sam's favorite band, U2. Our seats were in the nosebleed section, but we stood and sang and danced as if we had front row seats anyway. The encore song of the evening was "40," right out of Psalm 40:

I waited patiently for the Lord; he inclined to me and heard my cry. He drew me up from the pit of destruction, out of the miry bog, and set my feet upon a rock, making my steps secure. He put a new song in my mouth.

vv. 1–3 ESV

Bono waved his arms, inviting the audience to sing along. "How long to sing this song?"[1] Those words echoed inside of me. How long will I keep people out? How long will I keep my secrets in? How long will I live in the same song of despair, fear, and self-preservation? I've been singing the same sad song for so long.

On the drive home through the desert, my insides felt anxious. My throat was burning as if I had inhaled a shot of whiskey. My body was threatening me to stay silent. I nervously pinned my hair out of my face and forced myself to speak. The words if traced would have looked like a toddler's scribble. But they kept coming out. I told Sam all my secrets. And on the drive home, with my heart ablaze, I started to sing my new song. It wasn't beautiful or eloquent, but it was the truth. My secret stories were writing a new song over my soul. A song of freedom. A song of a girl refusing to live like I was already rejected. I wasn't going to force him to climb my walls any longer, I was coming out to meet him.

Just when I thought Sam was trying to find the polite words to break up with me, he pulled the car over. Maybe he was going to leave me at a bus stop or let me hitchhike home. The heat was sweltering. I wasn't sweating from the feverish Arizona hot spell, but the aftermath of vulnerability dump. He stopped the car, got out in a field of weeds, and asked me to marry him right then and there. He wanted me. Forever. He accepted me with all my stains and shame. He saw me and said, "I want her."

This is my favorite story because it's the one where I told a boy I liked all my secrets. In return, he asked me to marry him. He loved the girl hiding behind a billion brick walls. He loved me the way God loves me—by pursuing and accepting all of me for always. When I stay with my fear of rejection, with Christ, it's then (and only then) that I am able to find the acceptance I am looking for. Fear can so easily slip back in. I can quickly return to my tests and demands for more evidence. I've tried to get rid of my prove-that-you-love-me traps, but like cheap mascara after a long day, they're so hard to remove.

> When I stay with my fear of rejection, with Christ, it's then (and only then) that I am able to find the acceptance I am looking for.

I realized the gravity of my "if, then" issue when I threw a birthday party for myself that no one was attending. Birthdays are always tricky for me. I want to celebrate, but I don't want all the attention on me. It can be so awkward. Big number birthdays carry an extra amount of pressure because everyone loves to ask, "Are you doing something really exciting?" For my fortieth birthday, I decided to have a *Moth Party*. A Moth Party is when strangers and friends come together and tell real-life stories. People gather in bars, night clubs, concert halls, or backyards and share monologues of events that changed the course of their lives. From plane crashes

to a favorite teacher to the death of a parent, all these thoughtful stories together make what our culture calls a Moth Party.

With anticipation I clicked on the RSVPs. Who would be
coming to my gathering? Then there it was—more evidence.
Only six out of dozens replied yes. It was like the ground split
open and yanked me under by the ankles. I was dragged down
into that dark, damp cave. Instead of fighting against my giant
"nobody likes me" fear, I let it have me. I sobbed like a six-year-
old about a birthday party. I gave myself over to the belief I had
held at bay for so long—that not a soul cares if I exist. In the
dark chamber all the voices echo louder, stronger, and more
convincing.

Caves are inescapable. I think we all have them. We all have a
whole other world that lives in our personal underground. Our
underworld fears come up like hands out of the ground from
Hades and pull us below. We can only fight off the hands for so
long. Inevitably, we will succumb to the darkness and all that
lives down there. That night, when no one was coming to my
celebration, I sat on my blue couch and let the cave engulf me.
My tears weren't just from the lack of responses, but from the
evidence I had been unconsciously collecting for so many years.
Evidence proving how unwanted, by each person, I really was.
It was my *Moth* story. The story I had been playing on repeat,
always there, underneath it all. A story as persistent and bother-
some as a shoe tumbling obnoxiously in a dryer. The story I've
told myself goes round and round, again and again and again.

We all have these stories, don't we? Stories we are convinced
of. Stories that become the filters we use to see into every

situation. We look at others and ourselves through the lens of "if they cared," or "if they liked a picture on social media," or "if they see how hard my life is," or "if they show up," or "if they do and say the right thing," or "if they try to understand, listen, or make an effort"—then they love me. We have so many ifs and thens. We use so many tests to gauge our relational connectedness to other people. From our in-laws to strangers we meet at the grocery store, we play judge, jury, victim, defense, and prosecutor. From every angle we can accuse, cast judgement, and set a sentence.

We all live in our own imaginary courtroom. We interpret people's actions through a series of rigged tests and then dole out punishments. In every scenario, we can twist the story in a way that proves we were wronged, and the other person is at fault. But here is the thing about these tests: every test is set to keep people out. We want to be loved. We want to be loved so badly, but we are terrified of rejection, of being seen as an imposter or incompetent. We keep impossibly high walls. We send out riders to fend off any attempt of invasion. We turn every test into an ambush. We gather all the evidence and hold it up high like a banner. "See! You never really loved me. Look at all the things you have done or haven't done."

People can't prove they love us because the story we've told ourselves in the courtroom will always be stronger. It will always be louder than anyone's actions. What we need is a more powerful story. We need a story that rewrites all the stories. A new song. A song that sings a melody like a lullaby from a music box, tenderly opening the most vulnerable part of us. We must hear a song that outplays all the other ones. Fear doesn't undo fear. Anger doesn't undo anger. Sadness doesn't undo sadness. Only love undoes it all. All false narratives fall apart when love touches the loneliest stories we've lived by.

God doesn't stand outside the wall. He isn't inching closer trying to find a small crack to get in. He isn't trying to prove His love to us. All the proof we will ever need is in His pierced hands. His love rewrites all the stories with a redemption one. God is inside the wall. He is right there in the center of our rejection, always receiving us. His rejection makes a way for us to bear our own. We don't have to be afraid of it because His body took the brunt of it for us. The walls fall like Jericho, a miracle of the most magnificent proportion. People don't have to force the wall down or climb over it. We don't have to hide behind it. The barricade between us and others disappears. It's gone. We are always received and protected by Christ. Our significance is contingent on Christ, and never on the say-so of others. No matter what circumstance, situation, or trauma arises, we are always welcomed by the warmth of God first.

> All false narratives fall apart when love touches the loneliest stories we've lived by.

Because of Christ, our filter changes. We don't have to look at others in a stance of defense or attack to get love any longer. When we see others through the filter of giving and receiving love, we can live like the wall is actually gone. How can I give and receive love? Every interaction, every face to face, every conversation, every word spoken, this question remains—*How can I give and receive love?* How can I offer this person grace and further receive God's acceptance? When my acceptance doesn't hinge on their actions, I can love others freely. How can I show up for my friend and receive God's deep love for me at the same time? No more ifs or thens. Only one test remains. It's a test for me. Will I trust that I am loved?

We have to trust that people care even if they give love differently. We have to allow people the freedom to not love us perfectly every time. We have to give them the benefit of the doubt and trust they are doing the best they can. Unsafe people break our hearts over and over and wisdom will lead us when or if it is time to walk away. But we can't abandon relationships based on rigged tests. Both sides need to know the rules. We must stop playing a sneaky game of "if you loved me, then." Even if they don't step up the way we hoped they would, do the *right* thing, hug us when we are hurting, or respond the way we long for, it doesn't mean we have to disintegrate inside. We can hurt and be held because all of life is an invitation to give and receive love.

Wouldn't our lives look drastically different if we believed we were loved? We could stop the chasing, performing, and impressing. We could stop the manipulation, the traps, the complaining, the gossip, the stress, and the made-up stories. The mind games, the sleepless nights, the panic over saying the wrong thing, the jealousy could all end. We could release people instead of trying to catch them with a hook. When the name flashing on our phone screen threatens to swallow us, we can breathe again. We don't have to live in the courtroom any longer. Inside that made-up room are conspiracy theories that aren't real. We can walk out. We can be free. What if what the Father told the older brother in the prodigal son story is true for us as well: "Everything I have is yours" (Luke 15:31 NIV). The brother didn't need to work so hard to get affection, love, and acceptance, because he already had it. Everything we could ever possibly want and need is ours.

We must tell our love stories. Falling in love doesn't happen in an instant; it can be slow and scary. It involves stalling and getting stuck in reverse. We must let our stories be written under the penmanship of Christ. I know we are afraid. I know telling the scary chapters from our pasts makes us want to hurl ourselves off a cliff and volunteer to enter a witness protection program. I know everything in you is tempted to tell yourself a story of how people don't like you, want you, or care about you. Put on the armor of Christ because there is an evil one who wants to convince you to stay hidden, angry, and alone (Ephesians 6:10–11). There is a real battle, but it isn't with your neighbor. The real battle is to keep you cold and in your cave. But step into the light. Wear truth, hold on to righteousness, live in peace, pray at all times, stand firm in your faith. The more we wear this armor, the less we need to defend ourselves by our own strength. The longer we wear it, the more it becomes a part of us. When evil tempts you to go down dark pathways of thinking, put on your salvation story. Sing your new song.

> Wouldn't our lives look drastically different if we believed we were loved?

Literally, sing out loud until your heart believes your words. Slowly, you won't have to work to gain acceptance from others, but you will walk in your full acceptance with ease. It will be as though you've grown a new armor of holy skin.

That night when I cried on the blue couch, I tested people's love for me based on whether they pushed a button or not. But it wasn't fair because people do love me and even like me too. I'm forty, but still learning to believe this. My friends all came to my Moth Party. It was the loveliest night. My cousin Jessica made laab (Thai bite-sized appetizers packed with a punch of cold heat); Ashley came early and arranged the flowers; Kristin made the most heavenly chocolate raspberry trifle, peach cobbler, and cream layered cake. My sister skyped the entire evening from the Middle East. Sam froze watermelon chunks the day before and dropped them like ice cubes into gin, tonic water, and mint.

With quilts stretched out on the lawn, my friends shared their stories. One after the next we laughed, wiped tears, and sat amazed at the stories shared while sipping adult watermelon juice. Stories about getting lost on a hike, accidental kisses, and a night spent in jail. Bugs nibbled at our bare legs, and the glow of lights met the glow in my soul. I was so full. My soul was crowded with so much goodness there wasn't any space for more. All the excess joy overflowed onto a saucer. Not a single drop of joy was wasted.

Sam closed the evening with his story. He pulled out a piece of printer paper; I pulled my knees into my chest. I was attentive to every single sound and the way his lower lip slants right when he speaks, the sizzle of the citronella candles, the low hum of city noise, the anticipation surrounding each word he spoke. Sam's story began when he fell in love with me. He told our love story. The story about how he fell in love with me when I let him in. The day we drove through the desert.

When my party was over, I walked back inside slowly. I looked up at the sky with my soul as wide as a smile. Being loved is exhilarating, but believing I am loved is transforming. I slipped into bed next to the boy I've always liked. I remember his ultimatum and all the ultimatums I've given others. I'm learning to let go of my ifs and thens. I don't want to live behind my walls anymore or keep others away. It's a lonely place to live with the constant fear of rejection. I don't want to reject others before they can reject me. I want to focus on how I can give and receive instead of how I can take and get. How can I be awake to others if I am constantly rejecting myself?

Wake up, sister. Feel the entire weight of your body, bend your arms into your chest, stretch them out. Point and flex your feet. I know it is scary to step out of dark places. It's hard to believe you are loved because you've lived isolated on an island for so long. You've made people swim, row, and work hard to reach to you. You've kept people out on purpose. You are terrified of being rejected, and you have used so many strategies for safety. But take a risk. The world needs all of you. Your people need all of you. They need your wisdom, cultural perspective, and common sense. They need your passion, personality, and advocacy. They need your pain, sorrow, and silliness. They need your stories of heartbreak and heroism. Your community needs your humor and hope. Before you make snap judgments, stay curious because maybe there is another side of the story. Before you assume the worst about people's intentions, actions, or sudden ghosting on a text thread, ask questions. Stay soft and kind. Pray. Most people in your life aren't out to attack you, hurt you, or cause you pain. Remember the stories you've walked together. Even when your feelings attempt to tell you a false narrative, recall their character. Don't let your mind assume the worst. Perhaps they really like you, but don't always show up the way you hoped they would. Let grace be the greatest gift you give.

Stop giving your insecurities, fears, or pain the final say, but put all your security in the One who does. Please stop playing small. That's not humility; that's abandonment. Please stop pretending you're *just fine* when you are in desperate need of a friend. Please let people like you, because for goodness' sake, you are pure magic. Wake up to the expansive, wondrous, and freeing acceptance that God has given you through Christ. Sing your new song. It has nothing to do with being pitch perfect and everything to do with bellowing out the beautiful voice God gave you. Go back to the basics. Believe that God loves you, wants you, and knows you. Trust that people who say they like you really do, in fact, like you.

The night of my party, I looked above my head at the art piece mounted on the wall. Three words painted in magenta, aqua, and lemon yellow read, "I like you." Those three words have been framed above our bed for years. I wake up and fall asleep to them. I close my eyes and think, *Yes, they do. They like me.* I am accepted. No matter what, I choose to accept my acceptance.

3

The Luckiest

Wake up to more worth

My first job was at a care center for adults with severe mental and physical disabilities. I didn't want to work at a drive-thru or the movie theater. I wanted to do something that felt more meaningful. I suddenly felt grown up because I had to fill out that tax form, the one with all the boxes and confusing questions. Those W-4 forms still make me nervous. It's like I'm taking a test while the HR representative stands over me just watching and waiting for me to mess up. I was seventeen but felt like an adult because I could now buy my own candy, shoes, and concert tickets. I felt all grown up for applying, interviewing, and accepting a job where I got a paid vacation after ninety days. It's the same feeling I get when I actually have the receipt when I want to return something or remember to cancel an automatic monthly subscription after a free trial I signed up for. I felt proud of myself. I felt responsible. As a senior, I'd leave school after lunch and drive directly to the care facility. My job was to shower, dress, feed, and help the residents in the home to do the things they couldn't do on their own. I changed diapers, took them for walks, and helped the residents stretch their stiff muscles. Twenty-four adults lived full time in this particular home. I came to care for each one of them. Even though they couldn't say my name, our eyes knew each other. I'd talk to them, spoon-feed them, and tell them stories about Jesus.

A few weeks into my job, a new resident checked in. Her name was Sharon. Sharon was permanently in a wheelchair that she couldn't maneuver on her own. She had a severely arched back, and both wrists were paralyzed in a bent position. She couldn't talk, but she could smile. Her teeth were as poky as a succulent plant, but she smiled widely nonetheless. She always wore purple pants. Those were her favorite. Sharon was put on my caseload. I flipped through her file. I mentally noted how many homes she had been placed in—so many. Many of the residents move from facility to facility their entire lives. They celebrate birthdays without parents, presents, or parties. Holidays are lonely. Over time, many family members just stop showing up. Sharon was one of those residents who didn't really belong anywhere. While scanning her paperwork, I noticed something rather strange. It was noted that when Sharon gets upset, she likes to be sung to. Her favorite song was "Don't Cry for Me Argentina." I smiled. I liked her already.

Sharon got upset frequently. It was nearly impossible for her to communicate her needs, her pain, or her hunger. It was a constant guessing game. I'd be working with another resident and hear her scream from the other room. I'd run and check on her. I'd sit on the floor and rub her feet. Then I'd sing the famous song from the musical *Evita*, "Don't cry for me, Argentina. The truth is I never left you." Honestly, I only knew that one line, but I sang it over and over again until she calmed down.

Working there was hard. Yes, changing soiled sheets is an intense job for a teenager. But it wasn't the residents that made my job difficult; it was working with the other staff. Most of the time, I'd rather be with the residents in their rooms reading them books than with anyone I worked with. They constantly gossiped about each other, and anger oozed off of them like steam from drained pasta—hot to the touch. I kept my head down, did my job, and made sure I didn't get in anyone's way. I didn't draw attention to myself or ask for time off. I just did my work and clocked out at five.

I worked most of my shifts with George. He was a little older than I was. We went through orientation together. I was an innocent church girl who sang in the worship band. He smoked weed and dropped out of high school. Suffice it to say, we didn't have a lot in common. But I made it work. I invited him to church; he invited me to his friend's house on the weekends. We worked side by side most shifts. He did the heavy lifting, like picking up and transporting the residents. I washed their hair and picked out their new outfits. We bantered back and forth. He stood closer to me than necessary,

but this job required we work in close quarters, so I brushed
off my discomfort.

One afternoon, while in one of the resident's rooms, George
grabbed me. I shifted away awkwardly. I didn't know what to do.
So I laughed and went into work mode, shrugging off my shame.
When I'm uncomfortable, I giggle. I try to ease the tension. I
can't help it. It's the most natural response I have. I didn't know
how to feel. But when I left work that day, I knew what had happened wasn't humorous. I drove home quietly. I was confused.
I was anxious, and all I wanted to do was take a shower. Maybe
I was overreacting. Maybe it didn't really happen. Maybe, just
maybe, I was asking for it because I teased him about his casual
drug use. I decided that I would avoid him from then on. I'd do
the heavy lifting on my own. I'd make sure we were never alone
and the doors were always open.

The more I tried to avoid George, the more he was everywhere. Our shifts kept overlapping. He was assigned to the same
residents as I was. I didn't want to make things uncomfortable,
so I came and went as quickly as possible. I didn't make direct
eye contact or ask for help. I felt the tension, though. He tried to
make small talk. I'd laugh and busy myself away. I gave residents
their massages, changed their socks, and brushed their teeth.
I moved from room to room and checked on those who were
placed on my rotation. But I always found myself beside Sharon
with her purple pants. She wore them so much the polyester
was pilling. I'd sing her song, the one that soothed her. I'd sing
that one line over and over again. I felt out of control. I couldn't
change her circumstances or fix her body. I couldn't make the

wrong things in her life right. I couldn't muster the courage to make right the wrong that had been done to me. But I could sing. I could control this. So, I sang until her fingers relaxed. I sang until I wasn't anxiously looking over my shoulder. I sang us both into a calmer state.

I remained silent about the way my coworker treated me because I didn't think it mattered. I didn't think how I felt mattered. I shoved my feelings aside like food I don't like on a plate because other people had bigger problems. Was a sideways touch something to make a fuss about? I kept comparing the injustice in the world to the injustice that had been done to me. But when I pin myself up against the world, I will always lose. Somehow losing was all right with me. In some twisted, upside down, and backwards way, I thought I was better for being quiet. I wasn't worthy to come up for air, ask for space, or pick the restaurant. Martyrdom made me special. It made me valuable.

I was the one who was adaptable, easygoing, who could forgive and forget. I felt like I had to apologize for having needs. It's hard for me to believe

> I've often questioned if people want me for me or what I can be for them.

that people want to hear what I have to say. It's even harder to believe that they want *me*. I doubt anyone will show up if I were stripped of my reputation, creativity, or connections. I've often questioned if people want me for me or what I can be for them. I just don't think I am worthy to be loved. I can only be loved if I have something to offer. If I can bring support, a good time, or homemade guacamole, then I'm wanted. But if I show up with nothing—there's no way I'd be wanted. Singing to Sharon made all the hushed places inside of me feel safe. I didn't have to hide. In a way she could never understand, she was with me.

Music touches someplace deep inside of us in a way that nothing else can. It's magical like that. We all know this. We know how song, note, and minor chords have the power to hold, heal, and offer us hope all within a measure. It's mysterious that way. It comforts us that way. Music can melt our defenses like wax from a burning candle. It's so soothing. We can bleed and come alive in the same breath. It makes us feel safe like a hug from familiar arms. Even if pain is evoked, it doesn't stab us, but surrounds us. We fall into music. It catches us. It's on the inside and outside of us. Melodies give us air. Songs sung over us suspend our sorrow and ease our suffering.

Music can reach all the way down. Down past the places where words cannot reach, music gets free passage. Music wraps around all the unworthy places inside of us like a comforter cocooning us on a cold night. For me, music is like wine and cheese. It gets richer with time. The flavors never tire. The sounds never grow old. The soundtrack to my life would consist of a few dozen songs. The lyrics to these songs line my soul like the silky lining in my favorite blazer.

Singing over someone is a vulnerable position to be in. It's so intimate and even holy. You could be a professional musician or completely tone deaf, and the vulnerability is palpable. In a way, the more vulnerable the singing is, the farther down in a soul it touches. It's sacred. Music carries us through impossible situations. It transcends reason and vocabulary. It can take over and buoy us through unbearable circumstances. A single beat can strike our souls ablaze like a match. When we sing over others and when we sing to God, love is mutually given and received. It touches, perhaps, the innermost longings in our created beings. Through music our lost places are reminded they actually have profound worth. I think that's why the hymn "O Holy Night" is my favorite Christmas song of all time. "Till he appeared, and the soul felt its worth."

It's hard to imagine that God finds our souls valuable. It's almost impossible to believe that God would find so much delight in us that our mere existence moves Him to burst out in song like a flash mob at a mall. We have a hard time believing God sings over us in love. For many of us, God always seems to be teetering on the edge of disapproval. We have to keep Him from going over. We feel the need to constantly balance our behavior, good deeds, Bible studies, and cuss words so He doesn't just explode or leave us completely. God can feel big, distant, unreachable, and like a nice uncle who brings us gifts, but doesn't really want to be bothered. We expect God to bend over us rather than bend beside us. We assume God is like a disgruntled parent.

As a child, most evenings, I "helped" my mom do the dishes. I'd pull up an old wooden stool to the sink and splash water everywhere. She always reminded me to be safe, go slowly, and scrub the soap over all the edges. Every once in a while, a glass would slip through my fingers and shatter. I'd brace myself for the worst. I'd scramble to clean it up before she could see the mistake I'd made. But from the other room, loudly and almost in a song she would holler, "I love you more than that dish." She would promptly hustle into the room and scoop me up. No shame, no anger, no "I told you not to" eyes, but always protection and always love.

So many of us are bracing ourselves for a negative response from God. We approach prayer and relationship with Him from a defensive stance. But always, again and again, the song is sung, "I love you more than." God loves us more than what we can offer, more than what we've broken, hurt, or harmed. God loves us more than our best day of parenting, marriage, dieting, communication skills, or spiritual disciplines. He loves us more. Period. Always. We are braced for punishment, but He comforts us even when our bodies are stiff in shame. God hums a love song: "The LORD your God is in your midst, a mighty one who will save; he will rejoice over you with gladness; he will quiet you by his love; he will exult over you with loud singing" (Zephaniah 3:17). When we know this song, our souls are awake. God doesn't love me because of what I can be for Him. He loves me because I belong to Him like a child to a mother.

> So many of us are bracing ourselves for a negative response from God.

I've never heard God audibly sing. I sing to God. I join others in singing. But I can't say I've heard an actual voice sing over me the way my mom sang Sunday mornings from the second story balcony section of our sanctuary. My mom is a trained opera singer. At church her voice bellowed and bounced off the high ceilings. Heads turned and sneakily stared at the woman who could sing louder than the entire choir combined. You can imagine my embarrassment as a child. It's impossible to hide in a pew.

I've never heard God sing over me like my mom. However, I understand how God sings over me because of what happened to me years ago. Months before Sam and I got married, I was still in seminary. The wedding preparations were well under way, and I was trying to stay sane between studying and picking out centerpieces. Fear was slowly expanding in my heart the way a ripple of water widens without restraint, force, or willpower, but just steadily multiplies. I was afraid of losing myself in marriage. I had done so much soul work and therapy to get healthy. What if marriage changed all that? What if I lost myself in becoming one with another? I slipped into the empty chapel at my seminary and sat alone. The silence calmed me. Severe light lines sliced across the dark wood floors and ceilings of this little church. I'm not sure if I was praying with words or just feelings, but my ache spoke. My opposing fears and joy for the future felt as contrasting as the blinding light searing the walls of this sanctuary. I didn't want to get lost again. The thought of it was disabling me.

In solitude, I sat. In the silence so much noise surfaced. And as sharply as the sun burned through the stained-glass windows, a single thought burned through me. Like panning for gold, the dust settled. I saw what I had been looking for all along. If God was with me, I would never get lost. God is, was, and will always be with me. Healing never stops. Marriage, children, brokenness, abandonment, loss, tragedy, bad choices, or good behavior can never stop His face from shining in my direction. God always wants to grow me. God wasn't complacent about me; He pursued me. God wasn't putting up with me, God saw His creation in me. And the song came. A song I'd heard years ago by Ben Folds, "The Luckiest," came into my stream of consciousness. A raw, beautiful melody touched my soul as though God himself did. What if God didn't just love me but considered himself lucky to be my Father? Like a finger scanning a crowd, He stopped and said, "She's mine. I have to have her."

I've been fishing for worth everywhere my entire life. I cast my fishing line into every place except where fish actually live. I'm searching, always searching for the thing that will satisfy my incessant need for validation. Into the workplace, my boss's approval, and my parents' affirmation, I've tossed my fishing line. Through making a home, competency in the kitchen, doing things right, and providing meaningful information, I've tried to catch a bite. But all this effort is like fishing in my bathtub. Useless. Worth doesn't come from any effort of mine. Instead of fishing for it, I realize I've already been caught. A net vast and wide and safe catches me. God's song spreads into the deep and rescues me. I can choose to live in the obsessive slavery of catching fish in my jacuzzi, or I can rest in the truth that I have been adopted into God's family. God wants me for me and not for what I can do for Him.

Did I hear God sing over me in the chapel that day? No. Did the Holy Spirit remind me of His love through a song? Yes. Before my wedding, I hired a quartet to play during our ceremony. I'm sure they were prepared to practice Canon in D. Instead, I handed them sheet music for this song that God used to awaken my soul. On my wedding day, I walked down the aisle to "The Luckiest." God's song before, beside, over, and inside of me.

If you want to stay awake to God's love song over you, pay attention to the sound His love has made in your life. Remember the way the fisher of (wo)men picked you up when you had nothing at all to offer. Listen for His love. Hear it in the songs of redemption, the songs of hope, the songs of laughter coming from your children's lips. His song shows up in the gifts all around you and the imperfect, grace-abounding, impossible story you've survived through thus far. Through marriage, motherhood, and friendship, He awakens us. These relationships become a prism pointing us back to the presence of God. God's love is pursuing ways to grow our understanding of our worth. God's pursuit for you can be heard in your husband's calm voice, your sister's apology, and your friend's call just to check in. God's song sings through each relationship you have. Even in the most complex relationship, God is growing your worth. When those three dots on a text message disappear and your heart goes reeling, God invites you to find your value in Him. When your spouse's silence screams louder than his words ever could, God invites you to hear His love. When you can't

> If you want to stay awake to God's love song over you, pay attention to the sound His love has made in your life.

hear anything because of the storm of emotions wrecking your sanity, push play on the soundtrack God has composed in the world and in your life.

God created the expansive waters, the luscious field of happy wildflowers, the limitless landscape of hillsides sloped in a horizon of warm sand. He made women and men. He created us and said, "It is very good" (see Genesis 1:31). We will only see the good He sees in us when we look at the way He looks at us. So often we are turned in on ourselves. We see our flaws, flappy skin, and thoughts anxiously ricocheting around inside of us. We want to find our worth, but we panic by looking inside ourselves to get it like candy from a busted piñata. To see our worth, we have to see the worth God sees in us. We don't just see it, but we can hear it too. We stay with the song God sings over us, and we are awake to the intimate splendor of our souls' immeasurable, stunning, and significant worth. The most tangible reality of God's love for you is heard in His forever "I love you more than" song. A love so strong He sent His one and only Son to save you when you had absolutely nothing good to give in return.

I so easily forget that I have worth. I have value. I matter in a world that dictates that only youth, beauty, and political correctness make a difference. I don't have to live terrified to speak up a little louder. Pep talks, protests, and Post-its on my mirror won't give me sustaining worth. I want the kind of worth that grows up strong inside of me and doesn't just fall off after a few days like fake nails. No catchy phrase or trend can call out the worth in me. Worthiness doesn't just appear. It can't be coaxed, convinced, or created by more self-love chants. So often I listen to the tune of "work harder, prove yourself, you should be grateful, other people have it worse off, don't bother anyone, if anyone knows . . ." These songs become so familiar I don't even recognize the damage they do. I give them so much attention, time, and energy. I think if I listen to them, I'll be better and do better. I think I'll earn my worth. I think I'll earn the right to have a say, offer my opinion, have a seat at the adult table. But there is only one way out of unworthiness—listening to God's love songs.

Sister, wake up. Touch your ear. Touch your heart. What songs have you been listening to all your life? What false lyrics have you let into sacred spaces? Wake up to the songs Christ sings over you. Right now and always the songs come. Let them wake you in the morning and sing you to sleep. Over you, beside you, and calling you forward, God's love songs come. Songs of joy, patience, and love. Songs of peace, compassion, and kindness. Songs soothing, slow, and steady. As you listen to the songs of truth, the dark ones fade away. Your worth grows up from within you, unwavering and strong. Wake up to the symphony in Scripture. Hear the way He values you. Hear the way He is for you. Stop fishing for compliments, chasing a moving target, or searching for significance in a sea of hungry competitors. You don't need all that to feel secure inside. That's no way to live. What an impossible burden that is to carry.

You are enough. Just you, with your willing heart, cautious spirit, and complicated past. You are worthy to be seen, not because you stand out. You are worthy to be known, not because you know a lot. You are worthy for a second chance, not because you are better now. You are worthy to be loved, not because you worked extra hard, are good at helping, or for what you have to offer. At the very core of your being, you are adored. You have value because God said so. He is God and He gets to decide that kind of stuff. If you focus on finding your worth in what you do, you will always fail. Always. But if you remember the deeper love story God is growing in you, you will always find your worth no matter what you've done, what your circumstances are, or what you think you are missing out on. Hear the worth God sings over you. Let His voice and opinion of you be what holds you now and through the hardest times. Sister, stay connected to your true source of worth. Rest in His songs and let the worth you have in Christ be set free.

> At the very core of your being, you are adored. You have value because God said so.

Sometimes owning your worth starts with small, brave, steps. For me, it meant stepping into my manager's office as a seventeen-year-old owning her worth for the first time. I told him the story about being touched in a way that wasn't okay with me or anyone for that matter. My skin was blotchy, and my heart was burning like a jet engine. I walked away from that office shaky but empowered. When we walk in our worth, our whisper turns to a proclamation and our apathy turns to passion. Our life tunes into a song. A song with humility and elegance, sturdiness and serenity, empathy and valor. An investigation was begun, reports filed, and interviews done. Worth is contagious, not a limited resource. We can touch, awaken, and illuminate another's value when the mirror we hold reflects Christ. More staff members spoke up. More worth restored. More healing to come. More light transcending darkness. I walked away from that job a few months later a different person. I wasn't an adult yet, but I was growing in ways that some adults never learn to grow.

On my last day, I went into Sharon's room. She was wearing her purple sweatpants like she always did. Her head bobbed back and forth. For the last time, I sang to her. Sharon, this woman with silent courage, comforted me. A woman of true worth. I sang that one line over and over, "Don't cry for me Argentina. The truth is I never left you. . . ." I left Sharon that day knowing I'd probably never see her again. But she would never leave me. She changed me. She taught me that the song itself doesn't bring power. It's who the song is sung with and for that waters the small speck of dignity we have buried under a heap of rubble. I'd step out of that facility and forever see the world differently. I was a girl becoming. A girl on the brink of finding her voice. A girl hearing God's "I love you more than" song. He was transforming her shaky heart into the smooth skin of a cool stone. I was discovering my way. My worth swelling like a love song inside of me.

4

A Knock at the Door

Wake up to more humility

We made a humble offer on the house listed at 1066 Pinecrest Ave. I was certain the bank would take one look at it, laugh, and toss it out like it was last week's leftovers. If they didn't laugh, they would be annoyed that we were wasting their time. In 2011, several years after the market crashed, real estate took a slight dip. Houses were foreclosing as quickly as Blockbuster was becoming extinct. Short sales were as prominent as jewelry at a flea market. The housing market was in a momentary free fall. Houses were floundering and being swallowed up in a mudslide of missed mortgage payments. Through low interest rates and first-time buyer incentives, an opportunity arose for us to get a loan. The house on Pinecrest was bank owned, but I was in love with it. The floors

were torn up, the pool had toxic mold, the stairs were out of a
haunted house, but this little ranch house had potential. It had
a heart. I felt it. So, when we added our best offer to the thirty
other offers on the table, I prayed and panicked and started a
Pinterest board.

I screamed when our agent called that mid-September morning. We got the house. After signing what I'm sure was an entire
forest worth of papers, the house was ours. I painted our bedroom walls sea glass green, sealed up the dangerous stairs, and
moved our two little boys and four-day-old baby girl into this
house that would become our forever home.

When we were house shopping, we didn't take inventory of
the neighbors. The houses in the neighborhood all had their
own shade of character, the yards were well kept, and the street
was slow enough for kids to ride bikes safely. Everything looked
clean and welcoming. Except for a few potholes and the first
house on the left with a mysterious trailer on the property, it
was the perfect neighborhood.

This street is known as "Pill Hill." The first residents of
Pinecrest were all doctors who worked at the local hospital. In
fact, one can see the hospital from every house on the street.
Original lampposts from the mid-1950s line the west side of the
street. Weeks and months after moving in, we discovered the
heart of a neighborhood really comes alive through the people
that live there.

Directly to our left is Mrs. Harris. She's 91 years old. This
woman is fitter and stronger than most women in their twenties.
Scott, who owns a landscaping company, is always smiling and

lets us pick his lemons. I really like Emi and Eddie, who have the perfect color blue door, potted plants, and adorable dogs. I see them almost every day and they always stop to chat. We talk about current events, weather, and work. And then there is Lindsey. Lindsey, Paul, and their twins live across the street. They have a fruit tree in their front yard that is double the size of their house. Our street has a slow, feisty, and nice personality. We are laid back, but protective of each other. Come visit, but don't linger too long. Drive by, but don't drive fast. We are dependable and friendly, and we have each other's backs. If our street were an animal, it would be a cat: soft, but always slightly suspicious.

I met Lindsey the week we moved in. Her twins were four months old, and my Noelle was still wrinkly from the womb. I liked Lindsey right away. She was confident and well spoken. Both things I am not. Our friendship began with babies and grew with, "Do you have an onion, sugar, or chicken broth?" Lindsey is the kind of neighbor people dream of. I am the kind of neighbor no one dreams of. I have nothing to offer. I'm the one always needing an egg or advice or some sort of password. My kids often leave their bikes, shoes, and sweatshirts at her house. She is an endless resource. She knows all kinds of information, like where to get the best deals on cabinets, how to make the creamiest mac and cheese, and when to go to Costco at the least crowded time (Sunday at closing time. In case you were wondering).

When her twins were born after years of infertility, Lindsey struggled. I'll never forget a walk we went on together. The twins were strapped into her double stroller the size of a semitruck, and I walked beside her barely keeping up. She cried because she hadn't slept in months. She was exhausted and hurting and drowning. She said the words I'll never forget, "I feel like a failure." Then I cried. Because I knew this feeling. I know what it is like to be trampled by shame and suffocating in self-doubt. I know what it's like to think there must be something wrong with me because everyone else seems to be adjusting to motherhood poetically, except for me. I know what it's like to have dark thoughts, to be sleep deprived and angry all the time. There we were with our leftover baby weight, in our fourth trimesters, pushing oversize strollers and weeping in the middle of the street.

One time she was over, and in the middle of our conversation, my toddler completely lost it. He was crying because the banana I had peeled (ever so carefully) broke in half. "Bananas break," I tried to tell him, but there was no reconciling the death of our last banana, beheaded. I was so embarrassed that he would melt down in front of my friend. Nothing is more shameful than your poor parenting skills on display for others to see. I don't think he stopped screaming until after Lindsey left. The next afternoon, I came home to a bundle of bananas on my door handle from Lindsey. I cried. Grace was dangling from my doorknob.

Lindsey has a way of remembering important things like birthdays and what my kids are into. She knows my favorite tomato soup is from Nordstrom's Cafe. She found a spin-off recipe and makes it for me every fall, delivered in a mason jar and with love. When I had a baby, Lindsey made us pasta and fresh bread. She delivered the meal to my kitchen counter and proceeded to do my dishes. She insisted I sit and eat, while she soaked, dried, and put away my silverware.

One night I heard a knock on my door. It was late. Kids were asleep. I was retiring to bed. I heard the knock come again. I opened the door. There was Lindsey in tears. I was slightly worried. She said in almost a whisper, "Can I have a hug?" She didn't explain why or justify her bad day. She just offered her tears to me. So we hugged. Then she turned around and walked home, across the street, and up her driveway with the massive tangelo tree. That is courage. That's Lindsey. What you see is what you get. She is straightforward, humble-hearted, and real.

> I didn't want God to just be real; I wanted Him to be real to me.

I long for everything real, holy, and right. I've always wanted to be real, but it's hard for me. I'm good at figuring out who people want me to be and then being that. I have a tendency to maneuver around the truth just enough so I'm not lying, but I'm not fully being honest either. I'm good at bending myself into an image that will make you happy, pleased, or inspired. So when I meet people who are unapologetically real, it's intriguing. Since I was young, I've always had a craving for God to be real. I never questioned the existence of God. To me, when I look at creation, it's undeniable there is a creator. It's all too magnificent to think it was a mistake or mishap. I didn't want God to just be real; I wanted Him to be real to me.

I always imagined if I could see spiritual growth charted it would look like a straight diagonal line from the bottom left corner to the top right one on a page. At the top of the line would be heaven. There were people in front of me like pastors, elders, and smart people who understood words like *ecumenical* and *dispensationalism*. Behind me were new believers and well, people who were obviously sinners. Like an escalator, if I just stayed on the stairs, mindful of the gaps between steps, I'd eventually get to the top safely. My spiritual journey, however, has not been a straight line. It's more like a drawing by my two-year-old with bends, sharp edges, harsh colors, and parts scratched out. Although I've always wanted to have it resemble a peaceful escalator ride up to heaven, this has not been my case.

I've been derailed in my search for God by self-glory, being the good girl, and doing the disciplines by gritting my teeth and forcing a smile. Just stay on the escalator. Don't drink too much, kiss too much, wear tight clothes too much, or speak too much. Now exit the escalator. Ta-da. Welcome to heaven. It's almost too easy. Not so much.

My nondenominational church never talked about the Holy Spirit. It did, however, teach me a lot about the Bible. I was trained to stay in the lines and not have sex before I was married. When I was in college, someone invited me to their Pentecostal church. People were falling over, kids were running around laughing uncontrollably, and there was dancing in the aisles. Maybe this was the way to a real God. So I bought books, attended church services, and tried to speak in tongues. I spoke in tongues as well as I spoke Spanish. After five years of language classes, I could barely conjugate a verb. My "tongues" attempt was struggling to say the least.

For a few years, I met with a Lutheran pastor named Reverend Kraft. He played the clarinet and wore a robe. During our meetings he would clean his reeds and tell me about his anxiety. I liked that about him. He wasn't perfect. He would read litanies and recite prayers. I liked that too. He was a spiritual guru, but he was also normal. He would have been way ahead of me on the spiritual escalator, but when we met together it was almost like he was standing right beside me.

I think there is a little charismatic in me and a little conservative in me as well. I don't mind arms waving high in worship or the stand up, sit down formality of Bible readings.

But what I want more than anything is to be awake to God.

I want connection with God. I want to be real with God. I've found on my spiritual journey that there is always one crucial way to Jesus. It isn't just through expository study. It isn't figuring out the answers to baptism, the sacraments, or the equality of women in the church (although these are important). It isn't finding the church that meets all my needs. Megachurch, home church, small church, hip church, virtual church, and the church with the prettiest stained glass all fall short in some way. It isn't through tearing down other beliefs or being threatened by them either. It isn't following the celebrity pastor on social media.

True connection with God comes through humility. I learned that from Reverend Kraft, who started every one of our meetings on his knees. It was always the prayer, "Jesus, I believe, but help me with my unbelief" (see Mark 9:24). I want to give God my real self and be met by Him in return. I walk forward with a limp, open hands, and a humble heart. I have an earnest desire to please God, and like Thomas Merton, I have to believe that my desire does, in fact, please Him.

> My Lord God, I have no idea where I am going. I do not see the road ahead of me. I cannot know for certain where it will end. Nor do I really know myself, and the fact that I think I am following your will does not mean that I am actually doing so. But I believe that the desire to please you does in fact please you.[2]
>
> Thomas Merton

My humble offering of myself pleases the Lord. I don't bring anything fancy or fabricated. I bring me. I overcomplicate everything. I make "connection with God" about instruments, feelings, and formalities. I make disciplines regimented and difficult. I measure love by time and what I can tangibly see. I measure my worth by tracking a to-do list. I stay up at night anxious about my standing before Christ. I want to be right and know all the answers to feel secure. I am essentially walking down an upward moving escalator, getting nowhere, and worried the mall security guard will escort me out.

The church today is so fractured. Like cracked concrete on a sidewalk from tree legs stretching out farther and deeper, the church continues to split. We stand on issues instead of the peace of Christ. I've agonized over issues and lost friends. I've given up entirely debating the existence of hell. I've read books on sexuality, listened to podcasts on politics, and church-hopped because I was hunting for a spiritual hit. I've loved people who've held different beliefs on infant baptism and women as elders. I've settled on what I think is right and ached for those who stood on the other side of the aisle. But here is the thing: I could be wrong. In the end, I could actually be wrong on all these issues. I can earnestly pray, seek Jesus, and read what all the smart people are writing, but come to realize I was wrong the whole time. First Corinthians 13:12 says, "For now we see in a mirror dimly, but then face to face. Now I know in part; then I shall know fully, even as I have been fully known."

We only see a portion of the entire picture. We try to study, imagine, and figure out the full masterpiece now, but we are still looking into the fog. We fight, bicker, and break into new denominations. We draw lines, point fingers, and protect our stances. I'm tempted to throw my hands up in the air and give up. I want someone to just do all the work for me. I'll follow the one who seems the most confident and well spoken. I'll let the smart ones do the heavy lifting.

I've never felt smart. The right-brained people master the arts, language, and creativity; the left-brained people are brilliant at math and science. But then there is me. I'm mushy middle-brained. I'm average at a lot of things, but not really smart at one thing. Even though I made it all the way to a graduate program, I really skirted my way through school by perfecting my procrastinating skills and using my personality. I frequently find I have gaps in my knowledge. Oftentimes, people are talking about things like history or space or famous art pieces and I think, *I have no idea what is happening here.* I blink and smile and eat more appetizers.

When I was filling out paperwork for college, I had to declare a major. I thought being a teacher might be a good career path for me. So I searched thoroughly through the list of majors looking for Teacher. I thought it was weird that a high standing university had a Parks and Recreation major, but not a "Teacher" one. So instead, I checked Social Work. When I met my roommate, who was a "Liberal Studies" major, I asked her what she wanted to do; I finally figured out what the teaching major is called. (Come on universities, please don't make declaring a major the first test college kids have to pass! Most teenagers don't even know how to pick up their rooms.) I've learned to laugh at myself. That's me. Always figuring things out by stumbling along and pretending well—mushy middle-brained.

In my own insecurity, even after all my years of education, when challenging issues arise, I turn to the "smart" people for answers. Sometimes I believe only the smart people know more, understand more, and can comprehend complex concepts. Only the pastors and those with a PhD can translate the Bible. I just find the smartest person and follow them. But the Christian walk isn't about being smart. I don't think that word is even in the Bible. Following Jesus isn't about being the smartest; it's about becoming wise. In wisdom I seek truth.

So often I seek after proof instead of truth. I want God to show up, own up, and make up for all that is wrong in the world. I'll believe when I see the miracle, we get the money, the sickness stops, the answers come, or He makes the mess go away. I stand as judge and put God on trial. Somehow, I think I have authority to demand God prove himself to me. I want proof, but instead God gave me a dead man on a cross. Instead, He gave me forgiveness. All the terrible things inside of me are tied to that tree, and in exchange I am given air to breathe, clarity of soul, and hope despite all the darkness in this ever-dying world. Proof will never cast out doubt, only a dead man rising from the dead will. So, I put my hope not in the smart people, not in what feels nice, and not in my own authority. I put all my hope in the One who rose up from the grave.

I no longer think spiritual growth looks like riding a long escalator. I don't think finding God has anything to do with attending the "right" church, knowing all the "right" things, or doing things the "right" way. I think finding God isn't just for the really smart people who know Greek or speak in tongues. It's for me: the girl who isn't all that smart, forgets to buy eggs at the grocery store when that's the only thing she needs, and is halfway through life, but barely just figuring out what it means to actually live.

Spiritual growth looks like learning how to keep knocking. It starts with humility. The kind of humility that says, "I need you. I messed up. I hurt. Help me. Do you have a minute?" These prayers become the hum of my heart. Maybe if the church could start with humility, we might see the splinters turn to seams. Maybe connection to our real God starts there too, with just being human.

Sister, wake up. Wake up to your humanness. God's grace is most sufficient when we plan, perform, and control the environment—no. God's grace is most sufficient in our good defense, strength, and solid arguments—no. God's grace is most sufficient when we know the right answers, the pastor likes us, we have it all together, and yearly goals are achieved—no, not ever. God's grace is sufficient in our weaknesses. When we spend money we don't have, when our pants don't fit, when our knees touch the floor, when we forget someone's name again, when we can't make someone understand, when no one notices our absence, when anger leaks all over little ones, when we can't manage to stick another smile on our face—His grace comes in full force. When we repent, confess, and stay close to how insufficient all our efforts really are compared to God's glory, humility comes. When we embrace our lack, God meets us in love.

You can't force humility, but we grow into it. Sisters, when your real, honest, and passion-filled soul is vulnerable to the full light of Christ, humility springs up. When we come in contact with God's holiness, we are brought into humility. Stay humble as your spiritual journey turns, twists, and slows for speed bumps in its own beautiful and unique way. Sister, sometimes the smartest thing you can do is wait for wisdom. Ask for it. Depend on the Spirit to give you wisdom to guide you through difficult situations. Knock obnoxiously on the door, beg for wisdom, and wait. I know it can feel daunting, scary, and overwhelming at times, but remember you aren't forging your spiritual growth, but simply following Jesus as He forms you. Everything starts with humility. It starts with, "I need Jesus."

> When we embrace our lack, God meets us in love.

I want to be the kind of person who isn't afraid to knock loud and long. Even if I seem invasive, intrusive, or in the way, Christ says, "Keep coming." Perhaps in the weirdest way imaginable God invites me to be a bad neighbor, the kind no one wants. The kind of neighbor that overstays their welcome, never stops talking, and whose kids eat straight out of the pantry without asking. I don't know a lot, but what I do know is that I can keep knocking. I want to be humble like Rev. Kraft, who wasn't afraid to speak about his fears. I want to be brave like Lindsey, who asked for a hug in the middle of the night. God wants my scattered, needy, humble, and halfhearted thoughts. He just wants the real me. He receives me with a slight, growing smile across His face. In the same way the bank accepted our low offer, God takes my ridiculously small requests and welcomes me in, saying, "I'm so glad you are here."

5

There Was an Accident

Wake up to more hope

A few months after moving into our new home, our dear friends Emily and Arifin offered to make us dinner. Emily stood in my kitchen chopping spicy Thai chicken, while I mixed a tangy cucumber salad with red pepper flakes. I nervously peeked one eye up and asked if she was okay to talk about her sisters. "As long as you're okay if I cry," she said. I was. I listened, bouncing my little girl, Noelle, back and forth from hip to hip. Emily recounted that day in November so many years ago.

Years had passed since the accident. Decades even. It was on November 26, 1993, to be exact. I was thirteen years old when I walked out of the bathroom on a cold November morning. November, even in San Diego, has a chill, the kind you can see in your breath. My sister Malina was waiting for me. Her fingers gripped my shoulders. I was just barely awake. She said, "There was an accident. They both died, Jenni and Mylene. Both of them." I ran down the stairs, shaking, hot tears burning off whatever shiver I had felt just moments ago. I wanted to outrun her words. I wanted to run back to church, where I had last seen Jenni just days ago. I wanted to see her with her sleek black hair, full-faced smile, and long, skinny legs. I cried. We all cried in my family. But no one cried more than my sister Wanida. For it was that day her best friend, Jenni, died. Jenni was 16. Mylene was 24. Both were like beloved sisters to us all.

Mylene was the oldest and Jenni the youngest. Leaving one sister in the middle, Emily. Emily was married November 20th. Six days prior to the accident the sisters stood, shoulder to shoulder, on the stage wearing black velvet dresses, holding bouquets of white roses. In the span of two weeks there was a wedding and two funerals in one family. The tragedy is almost too unbearable to comprehend because it's just so horrific. Mylene and Jenni (along with one other friend) turned Thanksgiving weekend into a road trip to visit the newlyweds on their honeymoon eight hours north. The evening of the accident Emily hugged her sisters goodbye at a gas station. She woke up the next morning to the stammering and breathless words of her husband.

Emily told me about how Jenni slept right beside her on her last night alive. Their bodies spooned like when they were children again sharing a floor mat in Indonesia. Even though it was her honeymoon, she slept with her little sister for what would be her last night on earth. Emily and I both started to cry. She kept cutting. I kept swaying my girl. Emily told me she sobbed the entire way from Mammoth to her home in San Marcos. She was heaving and hurting, and her heart was dying as her husband drove without stopping. She had to get back to her mom. Her mom lost two of her babies in one swift, ugly moment of death. The night of the accident was as black as their velvet bridesmaid dresses. Who could have seen the stop sign? Two cars smashed into each other with the force of a lightning storm. At their funeral, when their bodies were lowered into the earth, Emily's mom had to be restrained from falling like dead weight into their graves along with them. I'll never forget the way she desperately clawed at the pile of fresh dirt covering up her daughters. It was as if the soil had arms and was strangling the air out of her. Death has a way of killing everyone.

Days and weeks following the funeral we gathered around my parents' dining room table. A table holding stories in photos, Kleenex, handwritten cards, and all our grief. Visitors and friends came and went like the holidays do that time of year— one after the next. But no matter what, there was always fresh coffee brewing. Between the waves of uncontrollable grief, there was also laughter. We all told the same story of the sisters but through different vantage points and laughed harder each time. I'd sneak away and look out my upstairs bedroom window. I looked past the withering jasmine hibernating for winter, to the orange trees scrawny and lonesome. Somehow the trees brought me comfort. I felt less alone. With pencil and white pages, I wrote my feelings. I felt connected. Through the words in my soul, I could find comfort and connection to the world around me. I felt like God could see me the way I saw the desolate trees. Through poetry, words hooked wondrously together, I felt like I wasn't dying inside.

My parents have four girls but hundreds of children. They adopted college students from around the world as their life-long love ministry. Our home was like a hostel for international students needing food for their bodies and God for their souls. The three sisters, Mylene, Emily, and Jenni, frequently slept on our couches, danced in our living room, and boiled noodles at midnight. My parents' house was a safe place for the lost to find Jesus. People were always in and out of our home, but especially on Friday nights everyone gathered to eat, worship, study God's Word, then play. We called these gatherings ICF (International Christian Fellowship). There would sometimes be upwards of 150 people in our little farmhouse surrounded by orange trees. Sometimes it would be so crowded that if you wanted to get from one end of the house to the other, it was faster to go outside and come back in through the back door than to go through the kitchen and hallways. There were so many people in our home you could barely walk at times.

Last summer, after forty-five years of generously opening their doors to college kids, my parents retired. My mom refuses to say *retire*. Instead, she says ministry will just look different. I like this about my mom. I like how she knows ministry isn't something you do, but someone you are. People from around the world came to celebrate their retirement—I mean, the transition in my parents' lives. People came from Thailand, Japan, and Texas. Friends flew in from Hawaii, Malaysia, and Maine. We moved all the furniture outside and taped photos up on all the walls inside. People paraded in and out of their home on the day of their "transition" to be with my parents. We had punch and a potluck and music playing in the background. There was always music. Ever since I was a child, every Friday night, I'd fall asleep to the kick and thud of a drum set. I'd hear fingers gracefully ascending and descending the piano keys. The floorboards shook to the stomping of students square dancing to a standup bass and guitar strum. But the greatest sound was the laughter. You could hear it from every room. Laughter, the invisible sound of happiness.

As the evening of the party came to a close, my sisters and I sang, "Welcome to the Family." At every ICF gathering we sang this song to move the evening from dinner to worship. At an instrumental section in the song, everyone stood up and greeted each other with a hug. This is when the laughter in our home was the loudest. People from all over the world, clothed in every skin color, embraced each other with smiling eyes. Asians, Caucasians, Blacks, Middle Easterners, disabled, misfits, young, and very old draped their arms around each other like long-lost siblings. Outside on my parents' U-shaped lawn, under the summer sky and Christmas lights that were never taken down, we sang for the last time the song we sang for over forty-five years.

I looked out over the faces of people I had considered my aunties and uncles, big brothers and sisters. There among the swarm of beautiful faces was Emily's. Her eyes were swollen from the constant stream of tears. Surrounding her were friends who had become like family since her sisters' deaths. People who stepped in, showed up, and stayed with her during the long nights of relentless grief. Several students came to know the love of Jesus because they lost Jenni and Mylene that fateful night. Their deaths brought so many lives to Christ. Now, in unison, like one family bridging the gap of forty-five years, we sang one final chorus together. The song we sang week in and week out, on this evening became our song of sorrow. It gave us room to feel the depth of our ache, gratitude, and sadness. Grief is so odd that way, isn't it? I felt both gratitude for what was and grief over what will never be again.

Grieving isn't a singular action, but slow and gradual healing. Sometimes grief can feel so big, daunting, and impossible, that many of us never grieve at all. It's just too hard. But when we grieve into it, like waves coming and going on a shore, grief feels possible. We grieve into heartbreak without the expectations of conquering but being loved in it. We write words like King David, who cried out to God in despair, anger, and belligerence. We scribble words on a page that catch our sadness like a net. We allow music to meet us in our mourning. Feel how the minor keys tap our souls awake. We let violin strings, solemn and lonely, soothe us in our quiet tombs. God is with us there. Through words, sound, and beauty, He creates a safe place for us to suffer.

Singing together one last time gave our goodbye safe boundaries. It was like a familiar wooden fence lining a pasture in the lush countryside. It gently guides everyone on the path in the right direction. We would need that picket fence because one week later, Wanida would pack up her four little girls and move to the Middle East to meet up with her husband, Joe. Because of his job in the State Department, they move every two years. Wanida has become very accustomed to transitions. She knows goodbyes. She knows the importance of staying heart, body, and soul till the very last moment. She knows how to be present, hold on, and then, let go.

The last time Wanida saw her best friend, Jenni, was a few days before the accident. She picked up a holiday position at the mall and Jenni visited on her lunch break. The mall was busy that day. Holiday shoppers were flocking to the stores right before black Friday. Their meal was quick, normal, and delightful. When it was over, they hugged and Wanida walked back to her next shift at Hallmark Cards. In the middle of the massive crowd, she felt something. Some*one* pressed on her soul, "Tell her you love her." She stopped and turned around. Peering through all the bobbing heads, she found the girl with perfectly straight, long black hair. Even though she was nearly one hundred yards away, she called out to her through the sea of frenzied shoppers. The water parted, making a way for the words to reach her. Wanida shouted, "I love you." Jenni's head flipped around, her smile rose as beautifully as ever, then she turned and went on her way. Wanida watched her until she disappeared. She would never see her again.

Something in Wanida's spirit knew goodbyes were important, necessary, and sometimes forever. God, in His grace, nudged her to holler like a teenager at a rock concert across the third floor of the North County Fair Mall. Those words that swept through a sea of people swept her up when all hope felt lost.

We need hope. We need hope that the windy river we are struggling in will eventually release us into the ocean. We need hope like the quiet dawn after a winter storm. We need hope to beat our hearts awake when we've lost the will to keep going and hope to keep breathing even when the pain is unbearable.

> Hope is a pause between two ideas. It gives us a moment to breathe and continue on.

If you have the smallest amount of hope, stay awake to it. Gaze upon it. Look for the tiny glimmer of light when you feel lost at sea. Hope moves us into the next moment. It gives us strength in the transitional spaces. Hope has no ending. It isn't like a period, but more like a semicolon. It's a pause between two ideas. It gives us a moment to breathe and continue on. The semicolon is a way of saying the story isn't done yet. When Christ ascended to heaven it was a semicolon moment.

Jesus leaves, but He leaves us with hope. This is not the end. *Don't be afraid; I'm coming back.* (See John 14:1–3.) When the pause comes, let us stay awake to the sorrow. Let us make poetry or music or lavishly splash paint on the walls. Let the pause make room for our grief to be held, explored, seen, and worthy of holding space.

Wake up, sisters. Tap your foot on the floor. Shift your hips. Relax your shoulders. Let all your air out, then receive it back

again. Wake up to the hope present even in the hollowest moments. Wake up to the living hope we have in Christ. A hope
that is connected to a person, not just a nice idea. Our hope is
attached to a human who lived, died, and rose again. Ground
your hope in the Gospel. Let the hope you cling to on the inside be made visible on the outside. See it. Touch it. Feel it.
Give hope color, shape, and creative expression. Write a story,
organize your closet, train for a race, feel grass tickle your back,
play the piano, arrange flowers on your table. Clear the path for
living hope to find a way into your lost dreams, broken home,
and cracked story. Send out a search party when you need help
finding it. Ask for a friend, call a counselor, listen to a sermon.

Sisters, wake up. Hope is rising even on the dreariest days.
When you find it, grab hold of it, talk about it, feed it, water it,
and let it grow. Find words that wake you up to the love of God
even when the pauses are hard, painfully impossible, and like
growing a brand-new heart. Hike high mountains and look out
long on the expansive landscape until you can catch your breath
again. Hold and be held between the transitions of goodbye and
hello. GOOD-byes matter. Lament and transition through life
with grace. Pull each other in for one more hug, lock eyes a little
longer, look in the rearview mirror when driving away. And for
no reason at all, scream "I love you" across a crowded room.

Emily and I wept remembering those winter weeks between
Thanksgiving and Christmas after her sisters died. She stirred
and tasted the peanut sauce to perfection, while I sliced the
limes. I've lived two more lifetimes since Jenni and Mylene
died. Emily has two sons, Joseph and Daniel, and one daughter,

Jaylene Hope. Her daughter's name is a combination of her sisters' names. They only know their aunts from the stories we tell and the wedding photos framed in their childhood home. Photos of when the sisters wore the black dresses and held white roses. When people die, they are never forgotten. I just think sometimes we forget to talk about them, even years later. But I still miss them. I wonder what they would be like and who they would have become. I imagine they would have been there with us, chatting about recipes, the cost of sushi, and how tiring homeschooling can be.

Noelle was fussy. I gently kissed her forehead and placed my hand on the back of her head. She won't understand what her name means for years to come. But when she is old enough, I'll explain to her what *hope* means and why we need it so badly. I'll tell her the story of my heart sisters who died one cold night in November. I'll tell her about the accident and how I found healing hope through dropping words into stanzas like seashells into a glass jar. Hope filling me up. Hope held me steady during the darkest transitional season of my life. Hope gives us the oxygen to keep going. My Noelle Hope was born November 26, 2011.

6

Thin Spaces

Wake up to more miracles

You are an evangelist," Sam said. Those words instantly made me feel uncomfortable. "I am not an evangelist," I insisted. To be honest, I can't even remember the last time I led someone in the "Jesus prayer." I can do small talk with other passengers on a plane, but I certainly don't preach to them. I don't have any radical stories about lighting up a revival. I walked up and down the beach once, passing out flyers about a church event in college, and I wanted to pass out. I was so nervous. Please don't give me a mic or ask me to defend my faith or explain Romans chapter 7 to your small group. Don't ask me how old the earth is, to explain the Trinity, or to predict when Jesus is coming back. I don't know the answer. Two things that can send me into an instant panic are playing softball and a faith debate. Both would painfully expose my incompetence. But Sam winked in an "I'm right" kind of way and went about making dinner.

I've known Sam my entire life. Well, since we were in grade school. We have so many beautiful, embarrassing, and funny memories growing up together. In middle school we were in a mixed doubles tennis competition against each other. He got so mad he chucked his tennis racket into a fence two tennis courts away. If it's not obvious, I won, and he lost (it). It was the same year of middle school Sam might have been referring to when he called me an evangelist.

The fog set the mood for that September morning and for everything that would soon come. A few dozen friends (Sam included) gathered around the flagpole at Hidden Valley Middle School to pray. Escondido, my hometown, means "hidden." Our town is tucked between mountains. From every corner of the city, you can see peaks pointing your soul skyward. Escondido sits hidden, wrapped, and protected by high, rolling hills. The outline of the mountains, if traced from far away, looks like people are holding hands, up and down, in one big circle around our city. This September morning weeks after school started, we did just that: we held hands. "See You at the Pole" is a nationwide organized day of prayer for students across America. With our oversized backpacks, hypercolor shirts, and side ponytails, we took turns talking to God around our flagpole. We prayed for our school, nation, and teachers. I noticed our principal, Ms. Edwards, circling around us like a spider spinning a web. She was watching in a suspicious sort of way before she interrupted us.

She informed us we couldn't pray publicly on campus. We had to take our stuff, Jesus, and our prayers to the sidewalk. Nick, the most zealous of us all, refused to go and wrapped his arms and legs around the pole. With a little convincing, Nick came with the rest of us to the sidewalk to pray before the morning bell.

Nothing gets our town more activated than religious rights being revoked by school administration. The separation of church and state is a hot topic that can divide a crowd as quickly as a hot knife through cold butter. We were twelve and thirteen years old, but we were going to battle against our principal and the school board. We had every constitutional right to stand around our flagpole and pray. If we didn't stand up, we were going to be walked over. So, I stood up—not like Nick with his limbs tethered around the pole, but with my voice. There was pressure and ill will from other peers on campus, but I was confident and unmoved by the side comments from other students.

I spoke to local papers, radio outlets, lawyers, and the channel 8 evening news. Before I knew it, other kids spoke up too. Slowly, our voices grew louder to the point where the school board gave us a slot to speak at the monthly board meeting. "See you at the board meeting" fliers were passed out like free lunches, and on a Thursday night, students and parents stormed the school board meeting. In a packed room with journalists, flashing cameras, and eight school board leaders on a stage sitting like judges, I spoke. I began by telling what happened to us that morning with the fog and my principal eyeing us like criminals. Student after student followed me. I wasn't afraid. I was grateful I had a voice that would be heard. We were ready to take our case straight to the supreme court if we needed to. Lawyers were hired and waiting. That night the school board ruled in our favor. We had the right to pray on campus. Our principal was wrong and apologized. A few weeks later Ms. Edwards called me out of class and gave me a personal one.

I'm not sure what happened to that girl who stood up to the school board. I'm still her, but years of disillusionment can wear down even the most outspoken. Years of doubt, leaders failing, and churches flailing have left my voice turned down low. I don't step up and out like I once did. I don't come out strong and preachy on any one issue. I don't think about moving to a developing country or giving all my belongings to the poor anymore. I've settled into a suburban life. I live for weekends, school breaks, and five o'clock, when Sam gets home from work. I'm not an evangelist. At least, not anymore.

I've never even heard God's voice. When people tell me they hear God's voice, I have two reactions: skepticism and shame. For the most part, I am not a skeptic. I actually lean more heavily into the naive and gullible category. If you seem like you know what you're talking about, I trust you. If you have a robust vocabulary, I will definitely trust you. If you add smarty-pants words like *data* or *analysis* to your defense, I'll never question you again. I don't have a gut feeling about people. If you seem nice, I'll let you drive my car, use my phone, or pay me back later. But when it comes to hearing God's voice, um no, I don't believe you. Then I swing the other way. Maybe you *did* hear God's voice. Who am I to say you didn't actually hear God speak? My thoughts turn inward; I wonder why I've never, in my forty years, heard God's audible voice. Shame. What's wrong with me? Why doesn't God speak to me like He did Moses or Danielle, the gal who cuts my hair? She can hear God's voice every day. I haven't heard God's voice, but I think I've heard God. Does that even make sense? God speaks to me. It's different from the way He speaks to my hairdresser, loud and clear, but I hear Him.

When I was younger God spoke to me at youth camps. I remember wandering off into the great wilderness and seeing God. I saw Him in the massive pine trees, branches bent like umbrellas over me. I could hear Him as the speaker spoke words that resonated in my soul. I came to know the tender love of Christ through memorizing Scripture and Bible studies with church friends.

As I grew, His voice changed. It came in conviction. My growing sense of right and wrong grew with age. When gossip was all that connected me to friends, when I kissed boys who could never love me back, when I lied to my parents, I could hear God like a resounding gong. This powerful force kept me from falling off the rails, getting pregnant, and going to the parties where the police got called. As I transitioned from single to married and into motherhood, God's voice changed. He became very quiet. He became faint and far away. Even when I strained to hear, there was only silence. Like a dull match, no matter how hard I'd strike, no flame would come. I felt abandoned. Looking back now, I think God was growing me into deeper maturity. God was growing me to trust Him even when I didn't feel, touch, or see Him. He was purifying my motives. I was growing from loving God for my sake into loving God for God's sake.

God doesn't speak to me audibly. Maybe He will one day. I won't stop hoping for it. But for today, I'll listen. I'll pay attention to the intentional, whimsical, and wonderful ways God creatively speaks to me. It isn't in a voice, but in and through knowledge of each other. I know Him; He knows me. He knows the intentions, desires, and details that only He could know. These are thin spaces. The moments in my life where I can almost touch God; He is so close. Thin doesn't mean shallow. Thin is the same feeling I get when I place my head on my pillow at night. My tiredness is gently received by fabric and feathers, and I fall asleep. I rest my head and my pillow becomes thinner.

Thin spaces happen when I let my guard down, just a little. I don't have to protect, preserve, or pretend. I can let go.

> Thin spaces are when my soul brushes up against the holiness of God.

Thin spaces are when my soul brushes up against the holiness of God. I am moving into a thin space when my soul expands. It's like a window is opening, and I know God is near. I can breathe easy. I keep the window open. I am known right here. It's a safe place. In the thinness, I am becoming full, connected, and alive. I encounter thin spaces when I watch waves curl on top of each other at the ocean with wind ushering salt water into all my senses. The peace of Christ is close. When bright light bounces off shiny stones smashed into small bits of pavement and I'm practically walking on glitter, the joy of Christ is close.

God knows the thin spaces that make my soul spring awake. I pay attention to these thin spaces because this is where I hear God. When they are close, I hold open the window as long as possible. I want to hear God. I lean in. God wants to hear me. I savor moments like these. When I'm eating sourdough bread with crackling, flour-freckled skin and chewy warm insides, smothered with sweet jam—I am close to God. For me, this is a thin space. I savor it. I savor God. I hear the slap-happy feet smacking the steps again and again and again. Children at play. I wake up to laughter. The other day my friend Sarah came over and taught me how to make wildflowers into crowns. The girls and I gathered lavender, daisies, and greenery from the front yard. We wrapped them in twine and let beauty balance on our heads like halos—a thin space. I grapple with my need for grace and my pride not wanting to receive it—a thin space. I prop the window open asking God for more connection.

The sweet honeycomb tiles, the bumpy texture of wall-paper, the sun spots peeking out underneath all the shade letting warmth fill up my skin—all thin spaces. The stampede of children shouting a thousand needs. I welcome them as God welcomes me—thin spaces. All these moments when my soul expands is how I can hear God's voice. I slowly slice heirloom tomatoes, their color as purple as plums. I don't move through the motion, trying to get to someplace else. I am here. It's a slow push and pull with a serrated knife, reminding me all of life is give and take. I lift, squeeze, and spin my daughters giggling with uncontainable joy—thin spaces. I feel paper, flat and fine through my fingers. Parchment whispering stories of when it practically touched the sky—thin spaces. When my soul feels the thinness, I am learning to prop up the window longer and breathe deeper. This is where I really pray. I pause my heart in moments like these. I believe God sees me. He knows my love for glitter on sidewalks, the calm sway of slender trees, and lying on quilted blankets during golden hour. He knows my delight for design, my dislike of stringy onions, and the sounds that light up my soul like my favorite song on repeat. He knows my story. He speaks over me.

Perhaps we all hear God's voice. We all have these thin spaces or subtle light-bulb moments when we just knew to take the job, dial the phone number, sign the lease, make an offer, hug the betrayer, talk to the stranger. Those choices were ours to make, but we were also led to the right one at the same time. Sometimes in God's severe mercy, we must face catastrophic pain without making a choice. We experience a heart death that actually ends up saving us from a spiritual sickness we didn't even know we had. These thin spaces, when we can almost touch God, led us to our husband, church, new home, best friend, or on the next transitional step in our story.

Thin spaces don't always make logical sense. People might even look at our choices and think we are crazy, like the other kids at my middle school did when we held hands and prayed. But when we listen to God's voice, it always aligns with Scripture and the character of Christ. We are afraid, but we also have peace. Something in us just knows. We know that we know that we know. So we learn to listen to God's voice and the way He specifically meets us. We listen in these thin spaces, in faith, knowing that God will once again lead us on the story that is already scripted. It's like reading a book and midway through we have an echoing feeling, "I've read this story before." Even when we haven't, we just somehow know it. It is familiar. Somehow, against all odds and common sense, a miracle happens. We get the job, meet our spouse, money arrives, sign the contract, conceive the child, get the check, or find the friend.

Maybe these moments are all coincidences. When we begin to believe God has lost interest in our lives or feel doubt settle in, we can look back at these thin spaces and start to explain them away. We can rationalize the parting of the Red Sea. Perhaps it was the wind shifting or tides changing that made the whole body of water split down the middle so they could walk on dry land. We can turn miracles into coincidences. But when you trace your entire story, it takes more faith to believe you've lived a million accidents than it does to believe in the mystery of good miracles. With so many miracles, it becomes impossible to reason them away. I think the gift is bigger than the miracles. The gift is the thin spaces. It is being held in a sacred space by God. It is hearing the sound, the texture, and the vitality of God's presence with us. I choose to believe thin spaces are miracles. God, who knows our deepest desires, passions, delights, intricacies, and personal stories, knows what we need. We were given sight to see God seeing us.

The miracles, big and small, are all a gift. We don't earn or gain or manipulate God into bending His will one way or the other. God does miracles for the sake of loving us. It reminds me of the blind man Jesus healed. After interrogation by countless religious leaders, the only answer he could give was this: "I just know I once was blind, but now I see" (see John 9:25). Don't we all have these experiences in our lives? We don't know why or how it happened, but somehow God healed, heard, rescued, saved, opened, comforted, redeemed, and did a wondrous thing. We were once blind, but now we see. Almost every single story in my life is a little miracle that came from a thin space. A place where my soul came in contact with God.

I can't stop talking about these miracles. They are everywhere. Every relationship, every job, every picture hanging on my wall is a miracle story. I never understood the passage John 21:25: "Jesus also did many other things. If they were all written down, I suppose the whole world could not contain the books that would be written" (NLT). But now I do. There were so many miracles it was impossible to document them all. Isn't all of life one dazzling, impossible display of miracles? We just have to lean into the thin spaces.

I want to hold open longer the window that keeps my heart close to the heart of God. I don't always have control of when the thin spaces come. Sometimes there are long spells of waiting. Dull, hard, and exhausting dryness makes my faith uncertain. We might even be tempted to believe that God has given up on us, is displeased with us, or has forgotten us. The waiting can be long. But when the thin space comes, listen. Lean in. Let God speak, and speak your soul words in return. Listen for the deeper story. God's story. Listen for your soul's voice that whispers, "I just know."

If I stay with these thin spaces, I will be awake to more miracles.

Wake up, sisters, wake up to the miracles God has done and is doing in your life. I know when life feels numb and dull it seems like God is doing nothing at all. But God is never done. There are always miracles in the making. Touch your face, bend your wrists, wiggle your toes, snap your fingers, and be amazed that God gave you a body. A body that moves you across the earth and enables you to engage in meaningful relationships. Feel your chest expand as you breathe in, be aware of the sweet smells around you, pay attention to your memories transporting you back to younger years.

Wake up. You are spinning on a massive-sized rock through outer space and somehow you can take a shower, recover from a cold, check your email from a glass rectangle you hold in your hand, read words on a page, and live a life filled with purpose. Take note of the vacations you've gone on, the landscapes you've gazed upon, and the music halls you've sat inside. Every relationship you have "accidentally" started. Your roommate in college, the random friend request you accepted on social media, the guy you said hello to at a small group, the other mom you casually talked to at Target were all miracle moments. I think God grins at these starting points because He knows what's about to happen. He knows how the story goes. You were at the right place at the exact right time, or your life would have gone a dramatically different direction.

Don't minimize. Don't forget. Don't fall asleep. Don't rationalize away the gifts God has given you. If you want to see God, stay awake to the miracles. Never stop talking about them, never stop smiling about them, never stop thanking God for them.

Don't worship the miracles; worship the maker of them. Sister, it is a miracle that Jesus radically meets you in your ordinary, normal, and slightly boring life and does incredible things. Sister, you are a living, breathing Mount Everest—glorious. Your mere existence is impossible without the imagination of God. Without your permission, control, will, or way, He wanted you here. Your heart beats; your body moves; your very bold, swift, and beautiful life is a miracle. Live that way.

I am not an evangelist like I was in middle school. I don't feel outspoken about my faith. I don't have all the answers. I don't.

> If you want to see God, stay awake to the miracles.

But I just can't stop telling people about all the millions of miracles God has done in my life. Miracles that just don't make sense. Miracles I can't explain with reason or logic. Miraculous moments when I was blind but now I see. The thin spaces keep multiplying like the loaves and fish. I can't stop marveling at God's miraculous love. I see it everywhere. His fountain of life flows through me. I see miracles sprouting up inside and outside of me. Impossible, beyond common sense, magnificent miracles are always present. Too many to even name. If I were to speak each one, I'd be breathless. Perhaps being an evangelist is simply saying what you see. If so, Sam was right, I am an evangelist. Maybe we all are.

7

Water

Wake up to more intimacy

was baptized two times. Once when I was six and again
when I was twenty-one. I realize this is not normal, but it
happened. It was not necessary, but I did it anyway. I was
baptized when I was young and didn't really understand what I
was doing. After I came to understand what a relationship with
God meant to me, I wanted to be baptized again. On a warm
summer night, before I returned to my senior year of college,
a crowd of fifty people walked down to my neighbor's pool.
My mom was there and my best friend. My dad and I were hip
deep in chilly water. With his thick Thai accent, he asked me
this question, "Do you believe that Jesus is the Son of God?"
I'm not sure if anyone saw me hesitate, but I did. I took a quick
breath and with eyes and cameras on me, I replied, "Yes." Then,

for the second time, I went under and came up. As my body was pulled down into the cleansing liquid and lifted up again, it was as though I was dead, and I was coming up new and alive in Christ. It was a declaration, a stamp, a seal that I belonged to God.

When I emerged from the water, there was shouting and cheering and lights flashing. I think I even splashed the crowd to punctuate the moment. But when I fell asleep that night, I was anxious. All I could do was think about that hesitation. Did I really believe Jesus was the Son of God? I guess. I think. Maybe. Yes, of course. Small seeds of anxious curiosity crept into my soul. But I turned the lights off, scraped my emotions aside, and went to sleep anyway.

I am good at a lot of things. I'm good at multitasking, taking pictures, remembering people's names, and networking. Sitting with people in pain isn't hard for me. I can still do all the time steps in tap and french braid my own hair. I am, however, bad at many things. I still count on my fingers and immensely dislike reading directions. I am bad at science and basic drawing skills. I'm bad at cooking unless it's spaghetti. I always lose track of my cycle (which accounts for some very challenging moments in my life and a surprise pregnancy). One thing I have always been bad at is holding on to me. Holding on to parts of me that aren't pretty or up to par is difficult for me to do. I swat away bad thoughts, shameful memories, and feelings that make me uncomfortable. I rationalize and devalue my fears. I abandon my feelings because of a million logical "shoulds" I come up with. I minimize my desires because they aren't important enough and quiet my voice because of my "what would people think" thoughts.

Getting over things is easy for me. I used to think this was an attribute. I'm sure at some point, I even bragged about it. I was so easygoing. I didn't get hung up on drama and girl spats. I was relaxed, fun, and not easily fazed. I was flexible, adaptable, and didn't care where we ate dinner or if you forgot my birthday. I was good at giving grace. But I did hold on. Like a dog gnawing a bone I held on to the ways I was dismissed. I pressed down the pain. I numbed it with Jesus talk and busyness. I don't think I knew I was even angry until I became a mom. This mellow girl turned into a grumbling maniac. I was mad at my circumstances, mad at the constant mess, but mainly mad that I couldn't just be happy, enjoy life, and settle peacefully into my new life stage.

Anger in motherhood is awful. There is nothing I hate more than when I dump anger out on my kids. It's ugly and heartbreaking and always ends badly. I've yelled so loud my throat was literally sore. When the heat on the inside and outside of me is rising, a safe place for me is behind the kitchen sink. I can put my frustration toward productivity.

Just today I almost lost it before 10 a.m. If one more person asked me for one more thing, I might just scream. I might explode. Children pull and yank and need me constantly. Hair needs to be brushed, bottoms need to be wiped, and screens in need of a password are pressed insistently under my chin. I just wanted a moment to breathe. I kept my composure. I planted my feet behind the kitchen sink. I squared my shoulders forward, head down. I dipped my hands into the suds. The water is like a restart. I put all my impatience into scraping dried egg yolk off breakfast dishes. I stacked, turned, and jammed the pans into the sliding racks of the dishwasher any way they would fit. Just like the junk drawer, I don't care how it looks on the inside; as long as it closes, I'm happy. My junk drawer and dishwasher end up looking a lot like my heart. I smash a lot of things in there, slam it closed, and then smile.

I wash and breathe. I trace my memory like the scar across my abdomen all the way back to the beginning. When did my frustration start? Maybe it has always been there, this low-grade irritation. It was there before the babies came one after the next. It was there on my wedding day when the caterer didn't arrive on time. It was there when I didn't make the team or when the mean girl bullied me. It was there when my sisters moved out one after the next, leaving me behind. My anger has been subtle and sweetly tucked under a pretty face. As I follow my anger all the way back to the beginning, I see it was actually sadness all along. Anger is a secondhand emotion to sadness.

> Sadness is easier for me to feel than anger.

Sadness is easier for me to feel than anger. Anger is big and scary and crushes people. I'd rather cry than scream. I'd rather ache than explode. I'd rather close the curtains than slam a door. Anger, for me, has always been dangerous. When I feel a hint of irritation, I don't really know what to do with it. I bobble it and bounce it around like a hot potato. Even when it burns, I keep it down. It gets bigger and more difficult to control. Then, out of nowhere, rage like lava spews up and scorches those I love the most. Everyone ends up burned.

But here, now, at the sink, I'm keeping my cool. I'm managing my emotions and overwhelming feelings. Then the littlest of hands pulls on my pant leg. I shoo her away with a slight grunt. She is whining and needy. I ignore her. My hands are soaking wet. My heart is on fire. I don't want to live like this, but I just can't seem to help it. I don't want to be the kind of mom who rages at the littlest request. But I am *that* mom. I am that kind of person. I bottle it up, then burst. I don't know how to express my sadness before it turns into anger. I don't know how to express my disappointment before it turns into resentment. I don't have a vocabulary for the feelings I feel because I am so quick to dismiss, set aside, or trample over them. Before I feel my feelings, I've already used logic to deflect a way out. My heart has a way of getting lost inside my head.

Perhaps growth of any kind requires making a place for my feelings to exist. Maybe it is less about a strategy and more about being honest and vulnerable with my basic human needs. Spiritual growth is about very child-like realities. It is faith like a child with innocence, tenderness, and even tantrums. It's learning to crack open my soul and let some of the inside stuff come up and out. I'm learning how to say things like, "I am sad. I am angry. I am hurt. I'm afraid. I don't understand. I'm scared. I wish." I wake up to the reality of my soul in this moment. The more I learn this childlike language, the closer to prayer I think I'm getting. As I get older, I'm learning that true prayer is really about getting younger. Because along the way, I lost the little girl in me. I shamed her voice, tucked away her thoughts, abandoned her true feelings. I forced her to grow up too fast. Wholeness is unifying my voice now with my voice back then. It's going back to that younger me and inviting her to come out. It's not leaving her in the dark or badgering her into being good. It's gently paying attention to the places I've bribed her to sit still. It's giving her permission to wiggle, play, and make mistakes. Prayer, now, is like that of a five-year-old. It is filled with a lot of rambling and run-on sentences. It feels foreign and irreverent, but I try.

I want my husband to come home from work on time. I want to shower alone. I want my son to obey. I want someone else to plan the meals and call the doctor. I want to sleep in and read a book and go on a walk by myself. I want to have a clean car and my kids to go to sleep when I say so. I want to hold a hot drink in my hands and finish it uninterrupted. I want to be a better mom, friend, sister, and daughter. I want to stop living under the pressure of a clock and an email response. Sometimes I am so tired, I don't even know what I want anymore. I just want everything to be different, especially me. I'm tired of me. Tired of my same issues and problems and complaints. I'm tired of being the only one who can't seem to manage being a grown up. I'm tired of my own inner dialogue. I exhaust myself. I'm certain people tire of me too. I'm too much. I have too many emotions and too little progress. But here I am. A tangled mess of what is and what I wish were. I can't keep up. I don't want to be afraid of being needy for help. Amen.

Childlike prayer isn't easy. It means I have to confront myself. I have to be honest. I have to give my reality a voice. I have to interrupt, raise my hand, and ask a question even if it means inconveniencing others. Sometimes prayer isn't just what I pray, but *that* I pray. I stumble through prayer to stay connected to my Father, counselor, and friend Jesus. Attending to my simple, confusing, and sometimes privileged dreams keeps me close to God and close to myself. I've spent most of my life following orders while abandoning my feelings. I think that's why as a child I was baptized without thinking much about it. My sisters were doing it, my parents encouraged it, I was intrigued by the mysterious wall that opened up into a jacuzzi on the back wall of our sanctuary, and Jesus was cool too, so I agreed.

I was always taught that baptism was a proclamation of my faith. Once my body went under and came up again, my faith was declared to all who stood by as witnesses. But I've come to believe baptism is more than an announcement. Throughout the Bible water is a symbol for purification. The Spirit of God hovered over the waters at creation. Like a mighty wind, God's power spread out over the chaos. When evil cursed culture, flood waters cleansed it. The Red Sea parted, making a pathway for slaves to escape. Christ calmed the storm, walked on the liquid as though it were land, and turned water to wine. With towel and transparency, Jesus washed the disciples' feet. Water and blood spilled out of His side, fulfilling a prophecy of who Christ was.

Water, again and again, signifying death and life. Water is a sign of transformation. From wicked to wonderful, from unholy to whole, from vile to valor—water restores. Water, the soothing reprieve satisfying my soul-gasping thirst. Water has the power to extinguish a wildfire and yet, pacify a burn. Water can calm a body and cut through stone. The components of one hydrogen and two oxygen can save a life or kill it. Baptism is a symbol of both: life and death. It isn't just a proclamation; it is a purification. It is a single act performed on the storyboard of my life, but it significantly transforms my everyday living.

Christ's purification in my life didn't stop when I was six, or twenty-one for that matter. Purification is always happening. Once purified, always pure. Baptism becomes the cleansing and the sanctifying process of Christ in me. Like a filter on a sink, baptism purifies me yesterday, today, and tomorrow. I don't have to scrub at my sin stains. I don't have to live in fear of being found out. I don't have to succumb to the lowest thoughts of myself. I don't have to protect my secrets. I don't have to drown in a pool of self-pity to get power. I have been made clean through Christ and purified through water.

Water makes a way for my childlike prayers to be received: water then and water now. Water is a constant reminder of the way God refines my very soul. Water in a rainstorm hugs the earth with nourishment—a reminder of my purity. Water in a shower replenishing my weariness with strength—a reminder. Water beading down my forehead controlling my body's temperature—a reminder. Water everywhere becomes a picture of God's purification. Even here at the sink, right now, with my daughter begging to be lifted—a reminder.

I didn't need to be baptized twice. My innocence didn't disqualify me. My youthful faith was enough. But when I went under the water in my twenties, it revealed my deeper fears. I wish I knew how to talk about my feelings. I'm still learning to believe that God cares about my longings and anger. That young voice in me is still there even though my body is growing old. I'm learning to listen to myself and speak up. I'm starting to believe that God wants to know all of me. I'm starting to trust how waking up to the little girl in me leads to more intimacy with Jesus. When my soul feels intolerable and embarrassingly immature, God makes space for me like a parent drawing a bath for a child after a long day. Water receiving. Water cleansing. God is close to the places I think aren't worth mentioning and offers me a drink. I am not just loved; I am understood and loved. It's personal. It's close. It's real. God receives my youthful ramblings as pure prayers.

I am not just loved; I am understood and loved.

Wake up, sister. I know you are angry. I know you are sad. I know you aren't who you wish you were most days. With a slight smile, inhale. Nod your head and exhale. Wake up to your childlike wonder. Wake up to the beautiful innocence of being a human with messy feelings that don't fit inside a personality type. The temptation is to put your desires to sleep because speaking them is too scary. In many ways, it is easier to just go through life unnoticed, not make noise or put up a fight. But it will come at a cost. You will end up living half awake. It means living as a hostage to the feelings you can't seem to control. The most devastating cost will be that you won't experience

God's up-close and personal love. If you don't wake up to the little girl inside of you, parts of you will always be asleep, cut off, and unknown. She deserves a voice, a say, and a little space to be heard, imaginative, outgoing, and shy. So even if it seems easier to stuff yourself away in a side closet, the truth is, you weren't born to stay hidden. Sisters, you were born to participate in a rich relationship with Christ. You were born to be loved. When you want to be awake to God's intimacy, touch water. Splash water on your face, drink a cold glass of water, jump in a puddle, swim in a lake, step into the rainstorm, float in a swimming pool, take a ridiculously long bath, and remember you are purely loved, inside and out. Wake up, dear one, you are intimately cared for in your innermost being.

I'm still learning to pay attention to my needs. I keep rambling through sentences until they make sense of my feelings. I'll talk as incessantly as my daughter tugging on my clothing while water runs down my arms beside the kitchen sink. Her needs aren't an inconvenience. She just wants me. I scoop her up and let her wet face and runny nose burrow into my sleeve. I fill our farmhouse sink up with water and soap and strip her down to bare skin. The water warms. I slip her into the basin with suds foaming up and around the edges, almost overflowing. With a cup I pour water down her back and rub her shoulders the way I do my temples when I have a headache, as though my touch can heal. The curve of her back is smooth. I twirl her ringlets around my finger and breathe a prayer. "God, she is lovely." I whisper words she doesn't understand into her ear: "I'm right here. I'm never going away. Take up all the space you need." God hovers over my chaos, bringing calm. God cleansing my rage with His ceaseless liquid resources. Even my tears are a reminder of His ever-present purification.

When I exhaust myself with, well, myself, water is always within reach. God knows how easily I forget how beautiful I am to Him. Water is a whisper of the pleasure He sees in me. I don't just proclaim my love for God, but He proclaims His love for me with every splash, drip, and downpour. The water slips off my daughter's lashes, a baptism of love right inside my kitchen sink.

8

Glass-like Glory

Wake up to more safety

My parents' Christmas tree lights are never unplugged. They dance day and night until the Saturday after New Year's. This year was no different. The lights flickered on the tree like fireworks over a lake, a happy sparkle bouncing back and forth over a backdrop of nature. Their tap dance on my parents' tree awakened my heart to joy. It was finally here. Christmas, with all of its hope and wonder and glory. The day I anticipated all year long was tomorrow.

All of the shopping was done, meals planned, and presents (mostly) wrapped. I hate wrapping presents. It's my absolute least favorite thing in the world to do. Some of my friends could wrap presents as a profession, but not me. I hate it. I'd rather potty train, put a fitted sheet on a top bunk bed, and vacuum

underneath the backseat of a car than wrap gifts. All the rib-
bon, glitter, and tape make me frustrated. I'm constantly losing
the scissors under the tissue and cutting the wrapping paper
annoyingly short or absurdly long. My back always hurts from
hunching over. Grinch alert. I know. I just have zero patience
to wrap gifts in paper that will be torn open without hesitation.
I've been known to wrap birthday gifts with a brown paper bag
and duct tape with no shame at all.

But this Christmas I was ahead of schedule. I was ready to put
on my Christmas pj's, watch *Elf*, and drive through In-N-Out
after the Christmas Eve service like we did every year for french
fries, double-doubles with special sauce, and milkshakes. My
little girls were wearing shiny black shoes, hair loosely braided,
and my boys were yanking at their neckties like they were having
an allergic reaction to being cute. My phone rang. The name on
the screen wasn't one I had expected. I silenced it immediately.
I was in the middle of gathering children, tying shoes, and pulling arms through painfully tight sweater sleeves. It rang again.
I answered.

Then, there in the middle of all the magic, my song stopped.
Like an earthquake at a wedding, tragedy interrupted beauty.
My cousin was screaming, "Grandma is dead."

Grandma Millie was 90 years old when she died of carbon
monoxide poisoning. She had survived the Great Depression
and had spent most of her life on the mission fields of India,
China, and Japan. This beautiful soul overcame a stroke, a broken back, and childhood trauma. Grandma died because someone forgot to turn the car off. The night of great expectation

turned into great sadness. Death brings out the best and worst in people. It makes everything that is raw and buried and quietly aching come alive. All the pain comes up. That's what happened when Grandma died. Everything broke.

Everyone traveled to Idaho for the funeral. From Alabama, Washington, Hawaii, and California we came. Like a storm of grief and loss and hurt we came. Dozens of us, children and adults, crammed into bedrooms and cars and filled all the empty spaces. I'll never forget the stoic face of my uncle who described finding Grandma forever asleep on the floor. I'll never forget the strangers who brought food, the fight between siblings, the snow, and the sick kids. My aunt Carol's breakfast casserole was reheated dozens of times. Each bite felt like I was scrolling happily back on my social media feed. A time machine of flavors transporting me to every single family gathering we've ever had. I'll never forget the kettle continually screeching as belligerently as our hearts wanted to, and the tea on tap poured out, soothing all our sadness. If anything can comfort a soul, it is my mom's chai. She stood at the kitchen counter caring for others by stirring tea, simmering milk, and adding the perfect blend of spices. My mom was hurting but trying to hold it all together.

One afternoon the pressure became too much and like the kettle, she shrieked. From the other room I heard her wailing. It wasn't just the grief from my grandma's death; it was a lifetime of grief. Grief from a million painful moments all built up. My aunt gently stayed with my mom's pain without fighting back. I wondered how many times she has been a pain holder for others. I wondered how many times my mom needed to lose it and just never did. Holding my daughter tucked under my arm, I listened and worried. I've spent most of my life trying to stop the screaming. Ever since I was a little girl, I've run into the room and tried to stop the breaking.

I was just a little girl with dark almond eyes standing in the shadows, hoping that my presence would make all that was angry stop. I would peek around the corner and see hurt hurled across the room. I heard doors slamming, tempers mounting, engines roaring. I saw pain like an avalanche cascading violently down the mountainside, swallowing up my loved ones like a monstrous force. I tried to stop it by being a bystander. I hoped my presence would make it all end. If I stood there

I thought I was strong enough to protect them from their pain.

long enough, maybe the war would cease. I thought I was strong enough to protect them from their pain. "Holding the arms that are supposed to be holding you" a counselor said once. For so long I have taken responsibility for emotions that aren't mine to take care of as a way to make the cracking stop in me.

I stood in the shadows, holding my parents' emotions even before I could stand at all. I stood there and took it, but in exchange I lost myself. I got lost in others' emotions. Their anxiety became mine. Their fear, resentment, and rage—mine, mine, mine. All the emotions exploded everywhere like the messy top of a squeezed toothpaste tube. But I didn't know that big emotions aren't always bad. Some things deserve big feelings. The loudest kind. The kind with crying and wailing and sobbing on the kitchen floor. I've spent so much of my life trying to fix painful feelings by standing in the corner, hoping my goodness could absorb all the bad. Here I was again, decades later, standing on the sidelines trying to make the screaming stop.

Some of us scramble into the brawl and get punched trying to protect the vulnerable ones. Some of us hide in silence as the destruction of drunkenness, debauchery, and downright evil march like the devil through the living room. For those like me, who have an addictive tendency to resolve everyone's pain, the worst thing imaginable is releasing myself of responsibility. I don't know how to leave people to their suffering. It feels wrong, sinful, cruel, and criminal even. I don't know how to let go. To do so feels like something inside of me is dying. My sense of internal okay-ness is dependent on others being okay. Even worse, I'm only at peace when others are at peace with me.

When emotions cooled off, my aunt took a nap. My mom went for a walk. Sam and I gathered all the kids up and went for a drive. Idaho, in January, is cold. Snow-covered streets and long stretches of nothing guided our escape. With the kids strapped in, I had a moment to feel the impact of all the sadness. Dusk was approaching. Darkness was chasing us. I could feel it closing in on all my pain. Then there it was. Something I had never seen before. Something so wildly beautiful it made my soul gasp.

A frozen lake. It was so sleek, pure, and poetic. I could hardly believe something so magnificent existed on this side of eternity. A lake once warm and rippling with summer moss, stones skipping, and fireflies was now a mirror reflecting earth's expansive white ceiling. I carefully stepped out onto the glass like I was testing gravity under my toes. It was scary and sacred. Pale pinks infused with swirls of peach, and gold streamers hailed lavishly above me. It was almost as though love was coming after me through a tapestry of touchable light, lasers searing me open. The dotted clouds looked like powdered sugar sprinkled across the sky. My soul was tasting sweetness.

Standing on this lake, experiencing all the death and grace and darkness inside of me made me feel alive. Beauty absorbing pain. Jesus stretched plastic wrap out over the face of the water. I stepped out onto what looked like eternity. A translucent walk of trust. God made a way to meet me. That day, with all my grief, He met me. On the cold lake water, with a song in the sky, He came. Jesus came out to meet me on this glass-like glory. I wondered if walking on water wasn't just a miracle from before, but a modern-day one happening right under me. My faith can feel as solid as a rock and as weak as water. Perhaps it is both. Perhaps releasing the people I love back to Jesus requires this kind of faith. It is hard and simple. It is hard because I must forgo control. Yet simple, because all I have to do is keep my chest pointed in the direction of Christ. I have to pry open my fingers and trust that Jesus will meet others that I love the way He is meeting me on this slate of ice right now.

I am learning how to walk on water. I'm learning that the slightest hint of conflict doesn't have to kill me or keep me up all night. I hate conflict. When it comes, I focus on how to dissolve it as fast as possible. Just put out the fire, bind the bleeding, caulk the cracking, make the tearing out-of-control feeling inside of me stop. But eliminating the feelings didn't actually end the argument. It just ended me. I think what I really wanted was to feel safe. I wanted protection. I needed good eyes to look straight into mine, hold my sweating hands, and say, "I know this is so scary, but you are safe. You are okay."

I just needed to know that when all the screaming was done, there would be a safe place for me. I am desperate for safety. When intensity rises, I'll grab on to anything to stay afloat. When I feel jittery inside, I get grabby. For most of my life, security came inside of me when I could secure the outside of me. I grab on to social media followers, a friend's comment about a meal I made, or my husband's touch to find sturdiness. Even now, I want to control the circumstances so my wobbly heart can feel safe. I reach for anything that will stop the rocking—news, food, money, time, influence, the next holiday, party, or paycheck. I grab on to more information, more theology, more articles, more podcasts, more voices, more sugar, snacks, or sex. But all these nets fail me. None of them can catch me. Instead, I just get more tangled up, pulled down, and turned in on myself.

The only safety that satisfies my soul is Christ beside me. When I stand with Jesus, like I'm standing here now, I am safe. I don't need to be more confident or have greater self-esteem or a better exit strategy to feel safe. I need to allow all my fear to find safety in the One who stands with me. I need to stay right here where I'm afraid the water will give way and trust God, in His grace, won't let me die. Here, He whispers, "You are safe. You are okay." I need to grow more comfortable with wandering into these scary places, the tender places inside of me, the fragile parts.

I've always had a wandering heart. And I don't mean wandering like the cool slogan, "Not all who wander are lost." I'm convinced that people who have that sticker slapped onto their raised truck or open-air jeep have worked through their middle-school anxieties. I'm certain those people have life figured out. They probably don't, but they have a lot more fun in life than I do. I'm the one internally curled up in a ball, rocking myself back into a semi-functional state, sucking on a lollipop, hoping someone else makes all my problems go away. No, I am the wandering *and* lost kind of person. I've always despised my fragility. I've been embarrassed by it. But I'm learning my fragility isn't a weakness. I'm learning there isn't something wrong with me because I feel partially disabled on the inside. It isn't a sign that I'm failing or incompetent. My fragility is actually a gift. It's what propels me to my true security. My fragility is what makes me so beautiful. It is what makes each of us so downright wonderful. It connects us. Fragility is vulnerability. When my fragility intersects with faith in God's love for me, I become more grounded. Conflict can come in any form, and I can withstand the storm. I am safe. I am okay.

The truth is, I always have been safe, but I'm just now starting to believe it. Maybe I need to make my own bumper sticker, "All who wander aimlessly feel miserable. It feels like you're roaming the long aisles at your local thrift store in summer, with no AC, and your toddler is rolling around on the dirty floor. You question your sanity for doing this outing during naptime. People are giving you side glances of horror as your other kids dash in and out of the racks. You feel dizzy, lost, and a bit perplexed about how you got here. But as you're rummaging through the coats, you discover an item that ought to be in a museum for holy, perfect, and beautiful jackets. All who wander are partially losing it on the inside. But all your wandering was leading you somewhere; you were on your way to gold." I realize this is a long bumper sticker, but I'm pretty confident that most of us are driving mom vans and not compact off-roading vehicles.

God is always safely leading me. Along the way, He is asking me to trust Him with the people I'm trying to protect. He is asking me to give everyone I love back to Him, where they belong. In vulnerable trust I am reminded that God is capable of carrying those I care about most in the world. The thought of letting people go makes my stomach hurt. But I want another way. Something deep in me believes there must be a better way. I don't want to be stuck here anymore. I want to feel air deep inside my lungs. I'm desperate for it really. People I love and people I've lost and people I don't understand can consume me. I worry about everyone.

People live in the middle of me. I wear them like a locket around my neck. My empathy can so easily become enmeshment. Intimate relationships, and even acquaintances, can be exhilarating, complicated, and agonizing (at times). I can't resolve the pain of my parents, or anyone for that matter. I can't heal others with my goodness, through a perfectly worded text message, or by stuffing my feelings. I can't. It feels like I am letting those I love most in the world drown if I let go. It seems wrong and mean and withholding to walk away. The guilt is overwhelming when I let people I love feel their own failures. I have watched marriages fail, children crumble, and friends slip away. I have to give people over to their addiction, stress, sadness, and fear. I have to give people back to pouring the next drink, clicking onto the next site, obsessing over body weight, and pulling away from their faith. I felt the sting of a fierce hand across my face and stood back up again because I thought my strength could resolve their rage. But it never did.

Releasing people isn't abandonment. It feels like it is, but it isn't. It feels like I am abandoning myself if I let people go. But, instead, it is rejecting the belief that I have the power to save them. Giving people back their pain isn't dropping them into a hole to freeze to death but inviting them to trust that the lake water is strong enough to hold them as well. It isn't throwing them on my back but extending a hand. We are both safe, not because of anything I've done, but because of what Christ has done.

So, I give back what was never mine to hold. I give people back their anxiety, fear, and big feelings. Their feelings don't have to become mine. We don't have to merge. For this moment, when my heart rate is rising, I release them. Each one of them I hand back over to Jesus by name: my mom, my sisters, my husband, my children, my father, my church, my friends, and all the people who have ever left me. They have never belonged to me anyway. They belong to Him. These people I love, the relationships I can't figure out, and those in my life I can't change—I hand them back over to God. They are not mine, but His. As I do this, I can breathe. I hear my voice. I can distinguish my own sorrows. With Jesus, there is room for all grief, heartache, and hurt to be held. I can share in the sufferings of others without wrapping them like a noose around my neck. I let God be God. I am learning that all conflict isn't mine to resolve. It's possible to be at peace even when there is relational unrest. I am still anxious, but I release, stand tall, and stare at the glass-like water before and beneath me. Perhaps all relationships were created to live right here—in the beautiful wide open.

This is love, and my needy heart wants more and more of it. Love is the gentle balance of holding on to people but also freeing them. Love is walking with others out onto the ice and trusting the water won't crack. It is dangerous and delicate. It is safe, scary, and heart-stoppingly holy. Loving people is like holding my breath and learning to exhale too. I have to release and receive. It hurts, but it also feels like something is healing inside of me. I'm letting my mom sob and my aunt be silent and my uncle face his trauma head on. I'm letting my daughter be emotional and my son be angry, and living with the sick regret that I didn't call Grandma one last time.

I'm stepping onto the fragile unknown. There will always be a little girl inside of me who rushes in with bandages and water when a war erupts. A little girl who is convinced that if she tried harder or sacrificed more, then white flags would wave. A sweet child who makes bargains and promises and believes tiny

> Love is the gentle balance of holding on to people but also freeing them.

lies that she is responsible to save the people who are sad. I've kept watch for so long, but Jesus has kept watch even longer. I imagine Jesus whispers to the girl in me, "I love them too."

Wake up, sister. I know you are scared. I know it isn't easy to let go of people you love. I know you wish there were another way. Close your hands and open them. Release. If you want to be awake to the trustworthiness of God, you must release your greatest treasures to Him. You must walk on water. Wake up to God's secure hand holding you. He meets you, heals you, and tends to you when you come in contact with His presence. You could spend all your energy, strength, and head space grabbing on to handrails that will only leave you limping. Stop grabbing for your phone, your youth, your pride, your witty comebacks to give you safety. Stop pulling on slot machine levers that consume all your time and money but never pay off. Stop trying to find security saving others from their God-given stories. You don't have to hold everyone's emotions anymore as a way to feel safe. Sister, you can't control or change anyone else. You don't have that superpower. The only power you have is to release people to the One who is all powerful.

Pay attention to your fragility. Welcome it. See that the shaky parts inside of you are inviting you into a healing story. If you push aside, silence, or shut down your vulnerability, you will constantly slip through life like a child learning to ice skate. You will only feel more frazzled and frantic. You will feel swallowed up and ashamed. What a dreary, heavy, and tiring way to live. Sister, wake up. All the safety you will ever need in this world is found when you let your fragile self be loved by God your Father. God, who safely holds the brilliant sun in the sky, holds you secure.

I am learning that my most fragile places are nothing more than a gift waking me back up to love. When I feel most frail, instead of frantically staying afloat gasping for air, I grab on to Christ for safety. I pray with all that is in me for love to heal hearts, including mine. I cry and close my eyes. I can stay on God's glass-like palm and walk forward believing He is, in fact, good. I let go and something in my soul feels like it's coming home for the first time in a very long time. I think about the lights on my parents' Christmas tree that never turn off and how they dance even brighter the darker it gets. A light flickers inside of me like the last light on the horizon fighting to stay seen.

Even as the shade closes on this day with the tea whirling and my mom's sadness and my heart shrinking, I am waking up. I am awake to the security God brings through the vulnerable walk of fragile faith. I am safe. I am okay.

9

Dish Towel

Wake up to more faithfulness

love the idea of ink scribbled on parchment. I love telling
someone I love, miss, or was "just thinking" about them
in perfect penmanship and poetry. I love the idea, but my
attempts to actually write snail mail have been wildly unsuccess-
ful. Evidence of this lies in the drawer of my office desk where all
my beautiful, blank, unsent DaySpring cards collect dust. The
drawer below that one has one hundred Costco Christmas cards
that were never signed or sent. The letter-writing process just has
too many steps. I have to find the perfect card, write it, find the
long-lost address, figure out the current cost of a postal stamp,
and then actually mail it. When I fail at one of these steps, my
entire mission is aborted. This is the reason I have one hundred
half-stuffed, unsent Christmas cards in my desk drawer from

last year. This might be a good place to mention that one year I doubled our Christmas card as a birth announcement and got my daughter's actual birth date wrong. I was off by two entire months (my poor fifth child).

Although writing letters isn't my forte, one letter I wrote changed my life. I knew I needed to write. I knew my words needed to be seen. I had to feel them. I needed to write slowly and feel their impact. I wanted my words to be alive, touchable, and not read through a screen. With my window open and the cool winter breeze stinging me awake, I scratched my pain onto paper. I safely sealed my heart into an envelope and sent it to my grandma. If there was anyone who could give me hope, it was Grandma Millie.

I was sinking and hurting and afraid. I needed to know that life was worth living. My internal light was fading; my external light was getting dark too. I'd seen so much loss and pain in the recent years that I began to question God, work, church, and Jesus. So many of my friends were abandoning their faith, and it felt like they were abandoning me. After working in a church, I started to see some real inconsistencies. Scales were falling off my eyes when it came to my belief system. I saw things that bothered me. Leaders had let me down, money seemed to be driving everything, and I felt like I had been a part of the problem. I felt isolated and struggled to find words to articulate the mess inside of me. If anyone could help me turn the light on, it would be my grandma.

I wrote about my scary thoughts, secret fears, and dying hope that anything good would come from living. Maybe it was a cry for help. Maybe it was my desperate attempt to be heard. But more than anything, I just needed someone I trusted to tell me all the suffering in the world meant something. I dropped my letter into the mailbox, labeled with her address, and drove away. Something inside of me was dying. I didn't know what else to do except lean on one person I thought would tell me the truth about what mattered most. She replied to my letter. I tucked her words into my Bible and deep into my heart. I carried them right up to the day of her funeral.

> I just needed someone I trusted to tell me all the suffering in the world meant something.

I'll never forget the long, lonely drive to my grandma's house after she died. I didn't want to drive to her empty house. I wanted to hear her feet shuffling down the hallway. I wanted to see her far-reaching grin bend up all her wrinkles into a million more happy little smiles. The lines curving all along her face mapping out a lifetime of glory and grief stories. I wanted her to pull me into her soft, round body and hug me with several quick back pats and laughter singing in my ear. I wanted her to start the kettle and panic glance around the kitchen looking for the milk that was, of course, sitting on the counter where she left it.

But today there would be no wide smiles or missing milk, only a vacant house filled with a lifetime of things imprinted by all the love stories she'd lived. We filed into the car and drove down a long, stark Idaho street to her house. I remember looking out the window, quiet. I was just watching the skinny, leafless trees and lonely houses spread out by acres of nothing. My sisters and cousins were chatting, but I didn't have words, just feelings—sad and angry ones, grateful ones, and anxious ones too.

Underneath the feelings was something I wasn't familiar with: greed. I could hear grumblings about Grandma's things: the jewelry, carved wooden statues, gold plates, and Grandpa's paintings. Greed is icky. It is ugly; it has a sound. Greed is as slippery as seaweed. It has a rationalizing and compelling voice. It persuaded me that whatever I wanted, I deserved. I felt gross for feeling this way, yet anxious I would miss out on what I had convinced myself Grandma would have wanted me to have. I just wanted something that was hers to be mine. I could hear this greedy voice inside of me and in the sidebar conversations.

When I walked through my grandma's home, people were swarming through the rooms. I could see the hungry eyes of people making mental checklists of the things they wanted. Somehow if they tagged it in their imagination, it was now theirs. I wandered into her bedroom. I felt the soft corner of her bedsheet. My fingers slid down from her lampshade to her nightstand and touched the stack of books. I turned the corner. I couldn't breathe. I heard a thud inside of me. This is where she died. Right here. The full weight of her body hit the floor until she fell asleep; her heart stopped.

I ran out of the room and sobbed hot, uncontrollable tears. I didn't want any of her things. I just wanted her. I wanted her to be here and to meet my babies. I wanted her to thaw a bowl of her famous Keema curry, with spice, peas, and soul. I wanted her to tell me everything was going to be okay the way she always had. I only wanted one thing of hers. Red-eyed and weak, I went into the kitchen, where my sister was holding a set of dish towels. I instantly knew which one I wanted. I wanted the ragged, holey, and wrinkled one. Grandma could have had it when she lived as a missionary in India, Japan, Orange County, and maybe even China. She probably used it to hold the saucepan when she stirred Cream of Wheat and to wipe the water puddles on the counter while preparing her instant coffee. This delicate, old, used dish towel was all I wanted.

This towel that recently touched her became my treasure. I folded it into my purse and felt the worn fabric between my fingers. This towel represented so much of who my grandma was. She was a hard worker. She loved with her hands by making meals, stacking wood, and sweeping floors. Day to day was a challenge. My grandma who sailed to India with one baby on her back and one on her hip gravitated toward a hard life. She stepped onto soil where her skin color stood out like white chalk on a blacktop. She saw suffering in the poor, the homeless, and children sleeping on dirt floors. She saw the dark heart of evil up close. The stench of sickness poisoned the city streets and crippled a nation. Death was everywhere. My grandma knew it, saw it, and moved closer to it. She lived through so much suffering. Yet, here, while I wept in her kitchen, her faithful service of love was comforting me through my suffering. I gripped the towel tightly, as though I were being held by her in return.

I hate suffering. If something is hurting, I'll do whatever it takes to make it stop. If I'm exercising and my muscles burn, I stop. If I don't like my job, I quit. If I don't like cauliflower, I don't eat it, for goodness' sake. I don't like fasting from social media, shopping, and (least of all) food. I don't like being put in a tight spot or accused of something I didn't do. I don't like when my kids are needy, really loud motorcycles, or water parks (how is running around in a wet swimsuit still a thing people pay to do?). If I have a slight headache, I pop a few Advil. I'm tempted to move to Oregon so I don't have to pump my own gas anymore. At airports I will always take the sidewalk escalator. To the travelers who opt to awkwardly balance their luggage, children, and cell phones for miles, you don't have anything to prove. Please take the moving machine with the rest of us. No one is impressed. I don't like anything that causes even a hint of suffering in my life. I hate it, actually. I can sniff out potential pain. I spend a lot of my energy avoiding hard things. If there is even a possibility of struggle, I'll go the other way. I spend so much of my life navigating around any sort of discomfort. I manage people, emotions, and my schedule to make sure no harm comes.

I crave an easy life. I mentally map out a pathway to the couch at some point every day. I'm suspicious of anyone who might ask too much of me or take up too much space. I want my life, on my terms. I want to control my suffering. I do this all the time.

> I don't like anything that causes even a hint of suffering in my life.

I don't have time for a flat tire or mold growing in the walls. I always feel a slight pressure to stay one step ahead of problems and ten steps ahead of any accusations. This pressure makes it hard for me to fall asleep at night. The list of what to do, who to call, what needs to be done never stops like the ticktock of a clock. The constant click of the small hand is like a critical judge kicking, flicking me, "Keep going, keep going, keep going." And I do. I dodge potential pain. Keep going. Be on time. Do the breast exam. Eat the good food. Use the better brands. Keep Band-Aids in my purse. Outrun any suffering. Feel the pressure. Let it be what pushes me. Don't let the pain catch up. What needs to be accomplished is what matters most.

Then Covid-19 hit. Everything stopped.

Our massive world slammed on the brakes and sent us all flying forward, seatbelts yanking bodies back from the deadly blow of the dashboard. Covid-19, like a semitruck, swerved dangerously out of control across the intersection and sent off a ripple effect of fatal collisions. Boom. Boom. Boom. I could hear them across the innerweb and inside my chest. The smashing, the cracking, our entire world crashing. The lights went out. A scary silence after a catastrophic accident hushed us all. It was eerie, like the terrifying lull between screams after a child gets hurt. The gut prayer is that another cry will come. Don't stop breathing, we beg our babies. Shock silences us. It grabs up all the oxygen. It's the quick, quiet gasp before the next howl comes. Covid-19 was like this; we were all left gulping for air.

Time stopped. All the pressure slowly released like a balloon letting out air. The clock demanding my attention no longer moved. I had nowhere to go, and anxiety came in like a flash flood. All the dams burst. All the pressing things from days before just didn't matter anymore.

All I had was time. My son became a teenager the day the world shut down. Empty chip bags and candy wrappers were still on the floor. My little girls played like nothing at all had changed. But I was changed. The pressure to do, do, do, turned into be, be, be. The one resource I was always short on was now limitless. Hurry eliminated. I was fully awake without the nagging pressure to stay one pace ahead of everything.

I walked my youngest, Mea, to the neighbor's yard to pick oranges. I sat in the grass; Mea pulled back the bumpy skin of the orange peel. The sun came out for a quick visit between the cluster of storms in our city. A storm was over us; a storm within us. The dark sickness crept like a wildfire through our world. Yet, here I sat with my little girl. No angst, no rush, no phone in one hand and keys in the other. She licked the sweet liquid sticking to her pinky. I felt it, tears swelling. Released. Then the words echoed like a gentle whisper amidst my internal chaos. *I think this virus is somehow saving my soul.*

There was nowhere else I had to be other than right there with her as she discovered sweet magic cupped inside an orange cocoon. I don't think I'd ever stopped like this before. I don't think I had ever really rested.

The gift tucked between large strokes of grief is subtle, but it's there. The gift of being here. It's the relief in knowing that the smallness of these sweet moments matters. I woke up to God and my girl. I woke up to the details. I had been missing long minutes of true eye contact. I had been missing the growing jawbones stretching my boys into young men, slow mornings, and my six-year-old stumbling to read through her storybook. During Covid, I carried the worry with my friends who could have lost their jobs and livelihood. I prayed honestly and slowly. Never before had I been more connected to my community. My people. With my little girl beside me, we watched the clouds move above us like a cinema in the sky.

This pandemic saved a part of my soul. I didn't realize how impossible my rhythm of life was. It was suffocating me. Peeling oranges with my toddler without any sense of productivity allowed me to be present. I don't want to miss this. I don't want to miss life because love is being cloaked in some form of hurry up, be more efficient, and don't make mistakes because, God forbid, we were late to soccer practice. I don't want to skip these moments because I convinced myself I could outrun heartache or keep ahead of any hurt. I know I intended to love, but maybe it wasn't loving. Maybe it was just me keeping up with the mob mentality that if I just stayed on top of everything, the easy life would come.

Suffering can't be avoided or evaded or undone entirely. Christ promises pain will always be with us in the world. I can't do anything to stop it. Covid dropped a bomb into my neat, perfect, fast-moving, just-get-to-the-weekend—world. Covid pulled back the veil and revealed how much suffering there really was. From racism to health care, poverty to politics, pain is everywhere. It's unavoidable. But I was just moving so fast I couldn't see it. I didn't want to see it. I thought if I hurried fast enough, I could control it. I could look the other way. Perhaps the goal isn't to outpace the pain but surrender to it. Suffering in one hand and my Savior's hand in the other.

When suffering comes, instead of moving fast through it, I'm learning to practice the discipline of slowing down. I'm tempted to run forward, fix, and find answers. I'm tempted to plow through the pain and just get to the other side. I'm quick to pass blame, accuse, or point fingers. But I'm learning to slow down. Pause. Suffering isn't going anywhere in our world. The real question is how can I suffer with others. I start by truth talking. One of the greatest temptations in dark times is to distort the character of God. I recount the things that are true. I know God loves me. I know God is good. I know God has given me resources to help others. I know there is a lot I don't know. I know I feel broken, helpless, and grief-stricken for those suffering. I know I also have a crooked heart that is self-seeking, self-focused, and prone to self-pity. When suffering of any kind comes, being really honest helps me take the first steps forward. It keeps me side by side with my Jesus. I know I can't save our broken world, but I can help hold some of the pieces. I know that I can be faithful to the tasks right in front of me. I know my small acts of service can bring comfort to a hurting world.

Watching my girl eat oranges, slowly, slice by slice, brought me so much comfort in all the unknowns. I wiped her chin, gathered the peels, and tied her shoelaces. I don't want to lose this peace when the pace of life picks back up again. I don't want to close my eyes and pretend bad stuff only happens to bad people. I can't cut out my responsibilities altogether (although my anti-scheduling personality might not be opposed to it), but I can approach them differently. More than ever, I want to lean into the life God has given me. I want to be here with my community, my children, and my church family. When the news is loud and the pain is unbearable, I keep showing up right here. When storms destroy cities and when governments collapse, I cry and donate dollars. When the poverty in the world is oppressive, I peel the potatoes and pray. When there is sex trafficking and religious stone throwing, I suffer forward through small acts of unseen love. One thing at a time. One person at a time. One act of sacrifice at a time. I don't need to heal, figure out, and solve everything. But I can love others suffering today by being faithful to what is right in front of me through service.

Suffering is real whether I want to see it or not. It started before my first breath and before my mom and grandmas. It began before my father and my father's father. My story is birthed from a long line of loss, abandonment, discord, and devastation. My story came from so many before me. It is a story of performing and pretending and the mounting pressure to keep up. My story is mine. It's unique and sad and underwhelming. If all I see is all the suffering in the world now and before me, I could curl up in a ball and just cry. But these stories sit inside a bigger one, a truer story of faithfulness. All suffering is cupped in a story of God and grace and redemption, the story of Jesus. Jesus, who took a towel, dipped to His knees, and washed the feet of His friends. He washed the feet of Judas. Jesus served each of them with eye contact, touch, and tenderness. Jesus cleaned the dirt from toe to heel of His disciples. He comforted them in the upper room as chaos was encroaching. Suffering was closing in on them, but Jesus paused to tend to their pain. He didn't stop the turmoil, but made His presence known in it. Jesus, the One who was beaten, rejected, misunderstood, hated, and hung on a cross, who died and came back to life again, suffered with others. Whatever pain I feel, I don't suffer alone. My wounds find comfort in His.

Suffering takes us down to a secret, sealed off chamber, a hidden floor in our souls. Suffering unlocks the door. It's painful, but what we find inside is companionship with Christ. I want to even say, "relief." The same kind of relief I felt when I watched Mea pick away at her orange peel, and I didn't have to rush anymore. Surrendering to suffering in me and in the world connects me more deeply and intimately to Christ's faithfulness.

Wake up, sister. I know it isn't easy to stay in suffering. It hurts everything. Blink your eyes. Tap your fingers on the table. Put your hand to your chest. Feel your heart beating. Twirl your hair between your fingers. You are a human with limitations. You don't need to hurry. The only place you need to be right now is here. If you fall asleep to your soul, your story, or the ache in the world, you will slowly be cut off from the love source. You will move, run, and push through life while something inside of you feels dark, disconnected, constantly distracted, and defeated no matter how hard you try. When you stay with suffering, you become awake to the grace, knowledge, and trust found with Christ. The ultimate dream isn't to live a pain-free, conflict-free, trigger-free life. It isn't to get to Friday or have a kid-free afternoon (as wonderful as those things may be). The dream isn't to check off the list and simply enjoy an evening beverage. Dream bigger, sisters. The best dream is the life you are living in right now. Can you see it? Be honest about your pain and circumstances. God can handle the truth. You can ask for the cup of suffering to pass from you like Christ did in the garden of Gethsemane (Matthew 26:39). In joy or in suffering, Christ is cultivating your heart into a home. Enter, engage, be present to the life you've been given.

Sister, you can't save the world, but you can be faithful to the world you've been given. Faithfully serve, love, and stay with the people God has placed on your path. Pick up a towel. When the world is dismantling, you have a part to play in the mending. Pick up a towel. Your hands will get dirty, your heart will be exhausted, your back will hurt. But don't miss a meaningful life because you are busy chasing after an easy one. Show up to the faithful work of serving others. Sisters, in the midst of suffering, pick up the towel, dip to your knees, and wash the feet of

> When you stay with suffering, you become awake to the grace, knowledge, and trust found with Christ.

not just your friends, but your enemies. When the world seems to be imploding, don't waver from showing up to the daily act of service. Stay on that path. If you want to be a part of healing work near and far, pick up a towel. Don't make excuses, don't try to prove something, don't make a scene—just serve. Take a deep breath. Slow down. Today, you can be the healing agent of comfort when you just show up and ask, "How can I help?" Stop running after an uncomplicated life. It doesn't exist. Stop trying to outsmart suffering. It is impossible. Stop avoiding conflict. It only makes everything more confusing. Stop living for a better life someday ahead. Someday is now. Pick up a towel.

My grandma had very distinct handwriting. Her cursive was large, extremely slanted, and the letters exaggerated just like some of the stories she told. Each word stretched wide out across the page. I'm sure the letter I wrote her years ago scared her. I was frantic, afraid, and saying scary things. When everything was out of control, she spoke the truth over me. She wrote a lot, but I only remember one thing. It would be the same words we stood and sang at her funeral. "Because He lives, I can face tomorrow."

> Jesus doesn't eliminate the story of suffering; He writes the prescription for it.

The only way through suffering is to walk with Jesus into it. One honest, wobbly, insecure, nervous step at a time. With Jesus, all hope, all joy, all purpose, all meaning—lives. The unknowns of tomorrow are made secure because of Jesus. Saying "Jesus" doesn't mask over suffering or make excuses for it. Jesus isn't a bandage to just stop the bleeding. Jesus bled to heal humanity from it. Jesus doesn't eliminate the story of suffering; He writes the prescription for it. Suffering is made possible because Jesus is alive.

I use my grandma's dish towel every day. It's as thin as a slip now. Every day when I catch the spilled milk, dry little hands, and do a thousand dishes, I am practicing the hidden faithfulness of love.

A faithfulness that holds me through life's darkest seasons. When difficulties strike me down or the world feels like it's collapsing, I believe God is hiding in the heartbeat of suffering. If I lean in, I will see Him. I wash, clean, and scrub the corner of the sink.

I dry the remaining water spots, fold my grandma's ragged dish towel, and hang it neatly over the sink. Hands clean, house clean, heart clean. I turn and look over my still and quiet kitchen. The hidden work of my hands matters. My character, faith, perseverance, and sacrifice all mean something. I want more of this moment. I want to be wide awake to the immeasurable importance of faithfulness. It means more than I will ever know for my life and the lives that follow. I hope one day when my life has come and gone the hard work of my loving hands will be the comfort my children will hold on to. Showing up with others in suffering moves the good of the world forward no matter what kind of evil exists. I don't need to clean up every mess, start a campaign, or get people to think right about something. I need to wash feet. I need to pick up the towel. I don't have to toil to avoid potential pain or live under the pressure to keep up. I can slowly walk right through it. I can stay with others in suffering and be awake to God's unrelenting love. I keep being faithful. I keep loving my community, stacking dishes, and unloading the car. I keep welcoming different stories, learning, and doing small acts of service. I keep doing what is unseen. I honestly pray. I want my soul to stay awake to the steadfast goodness of Christ, who suffered before me and with those hurting around me right now. I come back to truth. I turn out the light, humming, "Because He lives, I can face tomorrow."

10

The Monster Is Coming

Wake up to more peace

The monster is coming," the children scream, and like a herd of hippos they stampede down the hallway. The game goes like this: My kids hide under a blanket. They wiggle and giggle and squirm under their self-made shelter. Their shield of fabric protects them from the "monster." Nervously, they hush to themselves, "The monster is coming!" For ten seconds or two minutes they anxiously stay hidden for the monster to surprise them. This monster is typically another sibling, my husband, or when I'm feeling nice, me. Weeks into the California "stay home" mandate due to the Covid-19 pandemic, I was feeling nice. I played with my toddler and ten-year-old. We all held the woven blanket over our heads, our limbs like spaghetti noodles entwined this way and that, and chanted those four words: "The monster is coming."

I've lived so much of my life with a monster that was coming. It was just around the corner about to attack. I always had to be prepared and ready. I always had to keep loved ones safe and out of harm's way or at least aware of the approaching danger. Smaller monsters also emerged: what someone would think about me, gaining a few pounds, or an email I was afraid to open. Bigger monsters crouch, like financial debt, car accidents, potential plane crashes, the future death of a spouse. I'm good at coming up with monsters. Anything and anyone can be a monster. I can turn anything into something I have to control. I try to control how people perceive me, how to lie my way out of a mistake I made, and the right way to host a dinner. The monster, of course, is always a threat, scary, and will potentially ruin my life if I don't do something right away.

> I've lived so much of my life with a monster that was coming.

Perhaps one of the most paralyzing monsters in my life is conflict. Give me peace, give me affirmation, give me "we are good" winks. But the minute someone is disappointed in me or questions my actions or intentions, I come completely undone. The monster of discord is ugly, unpredictable, dangerous. I avoid conflict like I do gas station restrooms that have rusty, cracked mirrors, humming fluorescent lights, and toilet paper holders barred to the walls. The only thing scarier than conflict is the person who isn't afraid of it. To clarify, confrontational people both frighten and amaze me. I avoid them but also want to be them. I do a song and dance to try to keep my path clear of them. I do everything I can to live in such a way that no one can ever find a reason to pick a fight with me. So often I'm hovering above hard conversations. It's like I'm walking across a deck, barefoot, trying not to get splinters. Every step is calculated. I hold my breath. I try to be weightless. It's impossible. So, like the children under a blanket, I hide.

The year of Covid was marked with conflict, starting with Covid itself, then we had riots, racial injustice, party lines, political unrest, and the vaccine. The list went on and on. Would we host our annual Halloween party, meet for birthday dinners, or do the Christmas exchange we have done every year? If we gathered, how would we gather, where would we gather, and for how long would we gather? It was a complete nightmare. Globally, and within my immediate circles, disagreements endlessly came at me, one after the next, like a conveyor belt pushing a product through. As soon as I resolved one issue, another one seemed to loom over me like a dreaded date on the calendar. I wasn't able to keep up. I tiptoed through holidays, the election, and Sunday morning church just trying not to say the wrong thing and offend, hurt, or enrage someone. It was so hard. For anyone deficient in conflict resolution like me, 2020 leveled you or, more likely, buried you. Conflict makes me nauseated. I'm not sure how I made it to my forties without any emotional tools to handle disagreements. So naturally I Googled "how to agree to disagree." My search result read "drink more water." I was done. There was no hope for me.

I kept my focus on just powering through. I resolved not to offend, talk back, like a post, or recommend a podcast because it could cause problems. I wouldn't speak too much. I wouldn't speak too little. We could get through the birthday, get through my anniversary, get past the election, and Christmas. If I could just get past the new year, everything would be okay. If I could avoid eye contact with any danger, I would be okay. I wouldn't engage in hard conversations with people who might think differently from me. Just get to the other side. Then the Capitol building was stormed. I realized there is no such thing as getting through or past this. There was no avoiding conflict. Conflict is here. Perhaps it always was.

Conflict is everywhere; I've just been able to dodge it like a boxer avoiding a knockout punch. I'm afraid that if I get hit, I won't know how to recover. I'm afraid of what people think about me. I'm afraid of being found out or friendships falling apart. I don't know how to stay in a fight without being flattened. So, I hide. I've found the safe way through disagreements. I bury my head deeper and hold the blanket down tighter.

Hiding only makes the conflict monster bigger. I have imaginary conversations with people, and I have the perfect comebacks. The more I hide, the more anxiety creeps up my rib cage like needles on fire. Everything can cause conflict: death, money, education, entertainment, religion, parenting, retirement, where to vacation, and the sound by the front door. Anything can become a contentious, battle it out, I'm right and you're wrong disagreement. Conflict can exist between two opposing sides, but also between me and the world. I have low grade anxiety that at any moment, something horrible out there will happen to the people I love in here. It's always a me-against-the-world situation. I don't talk about it much because it can be embarrassing to admit the places where I let my imagina-tion go. I can come up with a masterful story for every scenario. I've practically planned out funerals, mapped out es-cape routes, and trapped the burglar in the hall closet. In my mind, I can take down two bad guys with the nail

I have a way of clinging to false security to make me feel safe.

file in my nightstand. Once I start the fantasy, it's hard to stop. I have a way of clinging to false security to make me feel safe. I think my exit plans will be enough to get away from all that is dangerous. I try to be smarter and faster and devise a better idea. I use tactics and spreadsheets and data to make my case. But after I'm done saving the world and coming up with the perfect comeback, it turns out that I'm still hiding. Only in my mind do I have control of all these big and small monsters; nothing can stop them from coming.

It was raining today. It had been raining for days. Like the "stay home" mandated by our state, the rain never seemed to stop. It was a Groundhog Day of sorts: screens, managing homework, and sweats. Every day was the same. I discovered restlessness and a restored longing for togetherness with people I love. I dipped my soul into the quiet surrender of unproduc-tivity and felt the angst to get things done. I didn't miss the rush, but I missed the rush of celebrations, crowded rooms, and restaurants with a constant hum of noise. I didn't miss the hustle, but I missed hugs. I didn't miss my to-do lists, but I missed the leisure of grocery shopping. I didn't miss doctors' appointments, but I missed my sister who is a nurse. We lived in familiar days of movies, forts, Legos, and dance parties, but we lived in a very different world. A world that felt foreign and ruthless and itching for a fight.

With the rain and the eerie illness that was caught through a small cough or brush up next to a stranger, I wanted to hide like never before. The rain kept coming down. The water, like a million people crying over a million people dying. The rain came. Water came down like a downpour. The tears of a humanity that was hurting came down. From China to Italy to the coast of Spain, we cried. From Seattle to San Diego, and New York to South America, we wept. We sobbed for the sadness of death, funerals over Skype, and for those isolated in hospital rooms. Like the rain, we couldn't make the virus stop.

The Friday when Jesus died, it rained. The earth rumbled an angry shake, the temple curtain split in two, the storm of death came and sucked love under. Mary, Jesus' mother, wept. How many mothers wept during Covid? Weeping for dead fathers and mothers and babies who died too soon or never arrived at all. I know weeping. As a mom, I know fear and heartache and "look both ways." I know "be kind" and "say sorry" and "it's going to be okay." But I don't know what it is like to watch my son die. I know the fear of it, but I don't know the agony of watching a child suffocate to death.

I'm not sure I've ever looked at Good Friday through the eyes of Mary. She didn't run or hide or take His place or tear her clothes off in anguish. She stayed. She watched the whips slash open His back, the mocking, the vulgar insults, the rocks thrown in rage. Mary witnessed it all. I won't stand for it if a kid is mean to mine on the playground. I don't put up with put-downs or pushing on the soccer fields. *Don't you dare touch my son.* When someone hurts my child, they hurt me. There, in the rain, Mary saw her son dying, and it was as though they were murdering her. She died right there with Him. It must have been that way. You can't watch your child suffer and not suffer too. Helpless to save, she stayed with Him. Mary's eyes locked onto His with the fiercest I'm-never-looking-away love. Her eyes were the only thing that could reach Him. She looked past hate and into love. She watched with immeasurable strength as her son, Jesus, unjustly died. Mary never stopped staring. The rain never stopped falling.

I knew Sunday was coming. I knew it would be warm and good and everything we had ever needed. But the hope of Sunday didn't erase the pain of Friday. I could only see the chaos outside my window and through my iPhone screen. I heard the branches banging repeatedly against the back door like the wind was out to aggravate my already fragile soul. I scrolled through media forums and felt the horror of careless words hurled back and forth. I pulled down the blanket tight. I tucked myself under and knew the monster wasn't just coming, but was already here. Right here in the rain and sun, I couldn't see through the thick clouds like steel covering the sky. I can't keep the monsters out because they weren't just coming, they were actually inside of me. I've spent my entire life trying to peacefully, gracefully, and with a smile on my face walk through a minefield. I felt a lot like Peter, who talked a big talk but ran the moment he was questioned. Then the imposter in me mocked all the more—*You are a joke, who do you think you are, liar, loser, fraud.* In no way was I like Mary, who looked love in the eyes and never looked back.

When radicals powered through barricades, waving "Jesus saves" paraphernalia, I watched stunned. When a noose hung like the devil's halo on the steps of the Capitol, I wept. I saw cheering and I saw chaos and I saw our nation coming undone. Everything felt sad and confusing. I needed to be alone. I pulled shut the bathroom door and waited for the water temperature to rise. I needed this. I needed hot water to clear my mind and wash down my frantic thoughts. I had no words, only flashing images in my head. The steam helped me breathe. I felt absolutely helpless and afraid. Then my little one poked her head in. My moment of peace interrupted by a girl in a pretty bow who wanted nothing but time alone with me. I invited her in. With the world falling apart around me, here, in our shower-storm, her presence was comfort. I got down on her level and she asked me, "Is your heart big enough for me and everyone else?" How do I tell her that she has my entire heart? This precious human is my everything. I would die for her if it meant she could live one more day. I tried to tell her that there was always room for her. She replied, "Mommy, maybe you have one big heart for everyone in the world, then you have lots of little hearts inside of that one for me, daddy, brothers, and sisters. We each have little hearts inside our big one." I looked in her eyes as though

heaven itself stood before me. "Yes, dear, I think you're right."
When I thought I needed to be alone, what I really needed to
know was that I wasn't.

When water rises and a flood of fears attempts to drown
me, what I really need is the comfort of loving company. I've
managed and manhandled my monsters alone for so long. The
stories I've imagined are always
me versus the world, me versus my
imposter, or me versus a conflict I
must figure my way out of. I forget
that God's heart is big enough for
the world and me. He has a heart
that can hold the entire history of
mankind and a heart that can also
hold just me. I vulnerably begin
to speak. I talk about all my monsters, the small ones I try to
squirm around and the biggest one right inside of me. I talk to
God about it all.

> When water rises and a flood of fears attempts to drown me, what I really need is the comfort of loving company.

I think I am so scared that if the really bad thing happens, I
will be undone to a point of no repair. I want to know that if
the tumor comes back, the divorce papers are filed, the rejection
text comes, I will be okay. I'm so afraid of not being okay. I'm
afraid of being sad, losing a loved one, and sobbing myself to
sleep. I tell Jesus about my fear of death and separation and my
kids getting sick. I speak about my fear of civil war, hate, and
raising my children without seeing strangers smile. I don't lean
on my strength or master plan or action steps. Those might help
me, but they won't ultimately save me. I wake up to darkness

and wake up to the love of God meeting me in the black cold of night.

I don't look away from God's heart looking at me. Sometimes it feels safer to hold on to anxiety than to let it go. I keep it as a backup plan. It's like the alcoholic stashing vodka under the mattress. They leave it there, just in case they need it. I hold on to fear, just in case I need it. It is another one of my tactics to control the uncontrollable. Anxiety isn't a choice, but what I do with it is. Sometimes anxiety is easier to feel than the lack of control I actually have. I pull my anxiety down over me as a shield. Living without control with Jesus can be harder than living with intoxicating anxiety. So, I'm tempted to let it stay and comfort me, instead of Christ.

Admitting I can't do a single thing to stop danger coming terrifies me. But when I stay *with* my fear of losing everything, *with* Jesus, I find it is the only way to get what I really want. Peace. When I talk to safe people about my doubts and my soul that dashes like a frightened deer at any sign of disagreement, I become sturdier.

My friend Becky says it like this: "When anxiety about tomorrow's uncertainty creeps in, you can make an intentional choice to include Jesus in everything you envision." I like that. I can imagine my worst-case scenario, but when I do, I allow Jesus in that scene too. When I imagine a break-in, break-up, or break-down, Jesus is there too. When I imagine disappointing my husband, Jesus is there too. When I imagine a war, a kidnapping, a natural disaster, a bridge collapsing, Jesus is there. He is all knowing, all good, and the greatest source of all love

I could ever imagine. The way to the deep down, all out, soul-satisfying peace I am desperate for is found when I am awake to the actual presence of the Prince of Peace with me: "For to us a child is born, to us a son is given; and the government shall be upon his shoulder, and his name shall be called Wonderful Counselor, Mighty God, Everlasting Father, Prince of Peace" (Isaiah 9:6). Jesus, the royalty of the world, conquered our monsters.

> Sometimes it takes minutes, hours, days, or what feels like a lifetime, but new life comes out of the tomb.

No other way awakens peace better than allowing the only One who is peace to be present. I let the peace of Christ invade all my imagination. The peace that withstood the echoing darkness of death is with me. A peace that endured the pain of the cross waits for me. A peace so subtle and familiar I know it like I know the salty air of the ocean. Admitting and accepting my lack of control is the only way to receive the dream I really want. Because more than anything, I want peace. I often live in the Friday Easter story. But I want to live like Sunday's always coming.

Sunday doesn't save me, but God does. Sunday doesn't stop the storm. It doesn't stop the heartbreak, or the anger, or the pandemic or death swallowing up earth in a single gulp. But it makes a way through the fire and fear and rain that doesn't seem to let up. Resurrection is right in front of me all the time. It is right there next to the monster and the grief of all mothers and the uncertainty of what could come. Right in the middle of the heartache is help. I open my eyes to the monsters inside of me. The ones that bully, prick, and taunt me. I let Jesus be there too.

I remember the way Mary had to look past evil to see love. Love is always there. She watched her son beaten, bleeding, and battling for breath. It's painful and scary and impossible to be present to such darkness. But when I stay and watch, I also see resurrection. Sometimes it takes minutes, hours, days, or what feels like a lifetime, but new life comes out of the tomb.

God wakes up the dead in me. Jesus heals with two words. He says to the little girl, "Wake up" (Mark 5:41 TPT).

I want to be awake. I don't want to stay under an igloo of fear my entire life. I don't want to miss the possibility of what life could be. I'm afraid of living a life where I'm always holding my breath, bored, and triple checking that I turned the stove off. I'm so afraid of wasting life on things that distract me from really living. It scares me to think I have to be a professional for people to take my dreams seriously. It scares me that I would rather stay stuck than have hard conversations. It scares me that I'd rather watch a sunset on someone's feed than in real life. It scares me when I'd rather sit with my phone than start a conversation with a stranger. It scares me that I avoid meeting people from different cultures because I am afraid of being uncomfortable.

It scares me that I have become numb to the loveless things in this hurting world. It scares me that I don't want to gather around a fire pit with friends, food, and new stories because it feels like too much work to make the arrangements. It scares me that I have come to a place in my life where I spend more time worrying about what people think about me than engaging in the absolute wonder at what God has made in the slender bend of sky between earth and eternity. It doesn't just scare me; it rattles me to the core. I look at who I have become, and I'm scared of who I will be in ten years if I don't start waking up from the slumber of half living I have been in. I am scared of living life, but I'm more scared of not living it.

Wake up, sister. I know how much you want to hide. I know the fear that comes with waking up. Relax your shoulders. Feel your pulse. Feel the fears that flash into your mind every day. Look at everything that is scary. Is it conflict, someone being angry with you, letting others down, or the bad thing happening? For a moment, let your soul feel nervous. Don't close your eyes to your anxiety, shove it down, or press it under. Don't cling to it for control. Don't pretend your monsters aren't there. We don't dare look away because if we do, we will miss Jesus. We'll miss the peace. You don't need external peace to have internal peace. Peace lives in you. When we stay with our monsters, with Jesus, we are awake to peace. "Peace I leave with you; my peace I give to you. Not as the world gives do I give to you. Let not your hearts be troubled, neither let them be afraid" (John 14:27).

> I am scared of living life, but I'm more scared of not living it.

Don't be afraid, sister. Don't lose your life to what-ifs and how-to's. Live awake to the reality that God has got you. If and when bad things happen, you will know His peace even when no reason can be found. That thing or relationship or conflict that has you in bondage, imagine Jesus is at the center of it. Imagine

He is nudging you awake: "I'm here, I'm here, I'm right here with you." He wakes you up from the nightmare. He pulls the blanket up. He brings you back to reality. There is a rich life ahead of you, a life of adventure, joy, and satisfying relationships, but you have to peek out from the darkness. Peace awaits you. Peace is with you. Sister, open your eyes. No disagreement, no unsettled situation, no trauma yesterday, today, or tomorrow has the power to ultimately hijack your peace.

The worst-case scenario of all is death. It is the single-most feared event for many people. Yet, Jesus went into death before us. With complete courage, He went to the cross and into death. He beat death, overcame it, and came out of the blackness with breath. Jesus went into our worst-case scenario and defeated it. We don't have to be afraid of it. What can death do to us? Now, when we die, we actually come alive. So, we fix our eyes on Jesus the way Mary did. We gaze into the invisible story beneath our present story to see Jesus giving us peace. We look through hopelessness to the One who is hope. No amount of conflict, fear, death, isolation, catastrophe, or cancer can ever separate us from God's big heart for the world and small heart for each one of us. Nothing.

Jesus says, "Little girl, wake up" (Mark 5:41 TPT). Love meets me here. Even in the rain, get up. The monster is here, but so is Sunday.

11

This Is Not the End

Wake up to more authority

The house was dark when we arrived home at midnight. Pitch black. Sam and I carried our sleepy and sluggish children into their rooms. After nearly twenty hours of driving, we were exhausted. Nothing is more draining than a road trip with kids. There's nothing romantic about a road trip when sticky car seats and smashed crackers are involved. The first five minutes are magical because the car smells as fresh as spearmint. Then all kinds of madness is unleashed. I spent most of the drive bent over backwards, retrieving snacks, cleaning spills, and adjusting the sound on the DVD player. But being gone felt so good. Our house was midway through a renovation and addition when we snuck away for a vacation. We had basically torn off the back of our house, added a bedroom and bathroom, and extended the kitchen. When we got home, everything was wide open. I collapsed into bed with my baby while Sam settled the rest of the kids into their rooms. A few minutes later, he crawled in beside me and whispered, "We have rats." Maybe it was the sheer tiredness I felt after doing handstands in a car for two whole days, but I shut my eyes, blocked out what he said, and fell asleep.

I am not ashamed to admit that I am scared of bugs, spiders, and California leaf-nosed bats. I am not even ashamed to admit that snakes, lizards, and crickets make me scream for Sam. I am, however, ashamed that I don't like animals in general. I am pretty good at faking my affection for dogs, cats, and the occasional pet fish. But inside, I only experience heart palpitations. My neck gets sweaty; I devise an exit strategy when I see anything furry coming toward me. I chew on my nails and do a weird nervous laugh to combat my anxiety. (While I'm revealing all my cards, I should add that I don't like Disneyland or guacamole either. It's criminal. I know.)

I try really hard to play it cool, but I'm just not an animal person (holding the rooster on the cover of this book was the scariest thing I've ever done). I don't like the feeling of hair moving on my skin or a wet tongue on my leg. I've talked to God about this and asked for forgiveness several times for my lack of animal affection and empathy. I can barely handle a raccoon in my front yard, let alone a rat. I hate rats. I can't even articulate the magnitude of my dislike for any rodent that is a relative of those dirty little creatures. Turns out that I hate them, but they love me.

The battle to rid our home of rats went on for months. We had pest control out dozens of times, set traps, and left out poison. I stuffed towels under the door jams, swept the floor free of crumbs, and left tea leaves in open holes (apparently this is the gentlest form of execution). One night we fell asleep to the sound of our piano mysteriously playing. It was our new roommates (the rats) scampering across the keys.

The next morning, I packed up our stuff and moved all seven of us into the upstairs rooms at my parents' house. These disgusting creatures drove us out of our half-finished home. It's like they were making a claim on our property. They were tormenting me like an older brother antagonizing his siblings for the sheer pleasure of it. They were out to get me.

I had never actually been tortured before. I am, however, the youngest in my family, so naturally, I was the easiest target for any form of pestering. One time my sister locked me in a closet and then forgot about me for a couple hours. That was the closest I've ever been to torture.

Perhaps there is only one thing worse than being tormented by fist-sized rodents—a root canal. Not a single pregnancy book warns moms about how babies in utero drain your body dry of calcium. Maybe the books tell you to take calcium supplements, but they never say that you need to floss one thousand times a day to protect your teeth from the damage done by these precious human beings. Nowhere in print does it say that your sweet little baby growing from the size of a pea to a pumpkin will ransack your body for this nutrient. Your cute little snuggly baby will suck all the calcium out of your body, and your teeth will in turn rot away.

After my fifth and final baby was born, my lower right molar started to throb. It started as a slow ache. It was somewhat of a phantom pain because it would come and go at all hours. My jaw started to clam up, and I found myself massaging my neck while nursing. Of course, there is never time to go to the dentist. It's literally the lowest priority in my life. After several nights in a row of waking up, teeth clenched, and popping a few Advils, I called the endodontist (the special dentist). I needed an emergency root canal. I drove across town in tears. I was terrified. I don't do well with shots or pain or plastic wrapped furniture. I don't like windowless rooms, poky instruments, or the sound and sight of a drill coming at me. I contemplated living with the unyielding pain in my mouth. Maybe I could do it. Maybe I could take Advil forever or never chew on that side of my mouth ever again. I was about to turn around and head home when I sipped some water, and my nerve was activated like someone took the end of an ice pick and jammed it into my tooth. With my arms shaking, I gripped the steering wheel and kept driving forward. The endodontist, without compassion, took one look at my x-rays and grimaced (again, not a good sign).

I needed a root canal right away or things would get worse. I started to cry. He blankly stared at me. I lay back in that sticky brown leather recliner. I cried harder. Tears couldn't get me out of this reality like they can when I'm trying to get out of a ticket. I wasn't sure if I could do this. I'm not brave or strong or a fighter. I'm a running, crawling-under-the-table, someone-please-rescue-me kind of a person. But even in my fear, nothing could compare to the pain I felt. My entire face, neck, and jaw were throbbing. I could barely keep my mouth ajar. I was trembling. I was in a panic. If it weren't for my children, I might be ready for the sky to open up and for Jesus to come back. I wanted this specialized dentist to be a therapist, hold my hand, and rock me to sleep. Instead, he snapped on his gloves and leaned over me. He looked me directly in the eyes and said the most terrifying words: "I will count down from three and then you will feel more pain than you have ever felt in your life. But then, I promise, you won't feel pain again."

With clamps fastening my teeth in place, my eyes widened. *Oh my gosh. I think he is going to kill me. For the love of God, I think this is the end.* He began the countdown before I could scream through the silver brackets propping my mouth open, "Three, two, one . . ." I dug my fingernails into my skin, my legs spasmed, and my back stiffened. He was right. This monster of a man was right. This was the worst pain I had ever felt. It was like he was screwing the sharp tip end of a knife straight into my exposed nerve ending and wrenching the blade deeper with all his strength. Raw, unrelenting, riveting pain sent a paralyzing shock wave throughout my entire body. Then, moments later, the evil dentist gently touched my chin with his thumb and said, "Keep breathing." So, I did. Slowly. In through my nose, then out again. Maybe he wasn't about to execute me, because he was right, again. I didn't feel any pain after he split open my fragile tooth with an axe. There was yanking, the surge and shrill of a drill motor, and the prodding of a hook, but no more pain.

After an hour of reminding myself to breathe in and out, he was done. My face was droopy and my body exhausted from clenching. The half-angel, half-devil dentist walked me to the front office. Cupping my face, I asked him what he did after he counted down from three. He told me that my tooth was so inflamed that he had to kill the nerves. If he didn't get rid of the source of my pain, it would only get worse. Infection would occur, and I would lose my tooth. Then he told me, "I don't tell patients what I'm doing. I want them to focus on my promise that relief will come." He had me there. I'm not sure I liked his bedside manner or his tactics, but he was right. It was actually better for me not to know the details. I just needed to know that the pain would be gone for good.

I haven't had pain from that tooth since. In fact, I've even gone back to that endodontist because five kids equals really bad teeth. I don't avoid the dentist or pretend anymore that my teeth don't hurt. I don't swallow pills or Google my way out of the reality that my teeth are in bad shape.

I have a tendency to run from pain. I adjust my meds or scoot around pain as quickly as a snowboarder dodges a tree. But pain untouched just festers. Pain isn't just pain. Pain is always trying to point me to something. The nerve endings get sensitive when the real wounds are being pricked.

All pain feels different. It has different texture, tone, and depth. Pain tells different stories. Some pain tells a sad story and some an angry one. There is another kind of pain we rarely speak of—evil pain. This pain is worse than rats and root canals. It's the kind of pain that attaches to pain. It has a hint of evil. Evil pain can settle into our stories. It festers and obliterates the inside of us. It laces our pain with a sour flavor. It can be subtle, but when you identify it, there's no denying it. No matter how much therapy we receive, how many books we've read, and how far away we think we've gotten from it, evil pain seems to stick. It leaves a bitter, unshakable, gnawing aftertaste.

I've been stuck in this kind of evil pain. I don't talk about it much because fear so easily attaches to it and mouths at me, "Don't you dare speak." Evil pain always *feels* the same. Always. It feels evil. The texture of evil pain feels like it's choking me. It can come as a faint whisper. It feels like taking a bath in tar, and no matter how hard I scrub, I just can't get clean.

We often don't talk about spiritual warfare because it feels like a taboo subject. In our world of science and physical evidence and common sense, spiritual warfare can come across as a little spooky. Isn't that the greatest evil of all? The kind that makes us believe it doesn't even exist or like we are a little crazy?

> We must be awake to the reality behind the reality. A battle wars for your soul.

Real evil exists. A desire to harm or inflict pain on self or others is evil. We know it because we've experienced it. We've felt this kind of evil pain that envelopes our center of gravity. A predator prowls around us like a lion, waiting to pounce on us at any given opportunity. A fallen angel, a being who was once so beautiful fell from heaven itself, and is now an enemy of God. He is out to harm the good work of the Gospel. The realm of spiritual demons seeks to destroy all redemption, hope, joy, renewal, freedom, light, glory, and peace that exist. A battle rages for your marriage, family, friendships, finances, children, church, government, and inner healing. The battle for your heart, mind, will, and spirit is as real as these words. We must be awake to the reality behind the reality. A battle wars for your soul. A strategy, a plan, and a scheme are at work right below the surface at all times, for you.

That's why it is so important to distinguish this kind of pain. Where a texture of evil pain is in your life, is where the battle is being fought the hardest. Evil pain slithers like a snake in dark places. Snakes strike fast. Their venom poisons quickly. Within minutes, swelling, itching, nausea, vomiting, and difficulty breathing occur. Your life could be going along normally, and evil pain can take you down instantly. It can hit you out of nowhere. Evil lingers in back alleys, quick clicks, false promises, and little white lies. It masks itself in wandering thoughts and dangerous dreams. It pricks us with rageful feelings and pours gasoline on our resentment. I can be doing dishes, and without forethought, scary thoughts will smack my insides with paralyzing fear. Evil pain pops into my mind without control or intent. My thoughts instantly spiral to dark places and before I know it, poison has entered my bloodstream. This spiraling-out-of-control feeling is evidence of evil pain. When dangerous, ugly, catastrophic thoughts drop like bombs into the deep end of my mind, evil pain is at play.

I've wished bad things on people. I've had conflict where the only way I could imagine it ever getting better was if there was a car accident or death. Maybe if I wasn't even here, everything would be better. Maybe if someone died, all my problems would go away. It's a very terrifying place to be in when you wish for a tragedy. I've been betrayed, backstabbed, and beaten up, and I've wanted revenge. I've wanted people to suffer like I've suffered. It's ugly. It's awful to secretly want harm to happen. Admitting it makes me want to gag. But it's true. I've let these thoughts take me to a dark world. When I tiptoe in this sort of darkness, I've lost. When I participate in hate, believe hate, wish for hate, deliver hate, self hate, I'm engaging with the demonic.

Evil forces have been sown into the fabric of our world. I see it in racism, our upside-down structures, and the jumbled mess of masculinity, femininity, and gender roles. I see it in the aggressive surge for more and more power like a pit bull that never eases up. Evil pain can be felt as an accusation. After listening to *The Place We Find Ourselves* podcast by Adam Young, I realized how spiritual warfare is always connected to shame. Shame holds me hostage with a gun to my head. Dark forces play on my shame like the rats running on my piano keys.

I've suffered with shame for as long as I can remember. My earliest memories include some sort of shame. I was awkward, different, and darker than the other kids. I've always felt a little off on the inside like a frame that hangs on a slant. Shame tempts me to blame. I blame Sam or the church or every broken system for my problems. I blame myself. I hold shame like a loaded gun. Like a gun, shame is holding me hostage with these words: "I should have known better." Shame bullets wreck, destroy, and fracture everything inside of me. I've taken the blame; I've dished out the blame. I've absorbed it. I've died trying to make amends for the bad things I've done or let others do to me. The shame whisper is sneaky and stealthy and sly. My relief comes through taking the bullets or shooting them at others. Someone must suffer to make the suffering stop. The other temptation is to resolve shame by pointing my gun at others. Someone has to take the hit for it. This temptation is so subtle, strong, and mesmerizing. I'm tempted to take a bite into that apple and then blame Eve or even God the way Adam did: "The woman *you* gave me made me do it" (see Genesis 3:12). I blame God.

I can turn the accuser into the scapegoat for my shame. The accuser can be anything or anyone. It can be a person, nation, or people group. It can be a brand, president, company, or religious group. If I can blame my shame on someone else, I can escape the feeling of shame entirely. I can blame my shame on an institution—*the church made me feel bad*. I can pass off my blame onto culture—*those people made me do it*. I can pin my shame on a person—*it's her fault or his fault that I feel so miserable inside*. I can turn my evil desires into green lights, insisting that it's my turn to go after the things I want. In essence, *How dare anyone or anything get in the way of my desires.* Those dangerous desires come like the serpent in the garden: *Maybe leaving my husband is a good thing. It's my turn to pursue my dreams no matter what the cost. I can bend the rules just a little. No one will ever find out. I'll just watch it one more time. It's just a little lie. What I did was bad, but what they did was worse. I wish this difficult person in my life would just disappear or that high official would be assassinated. I want that person's life, spouse, career, looks. I can use someone to get what I want in the name of friendship.* We convince ourselves that the thoughts we've had in the dark aren't meant to be silenced but to be our cheerleaders.

Tantalizing voices in the darkness turn evil into good by getting rid of shame altogether. One of the scariest things I see in our culture today is the dangerous elimination of shame. That thing that you feel bad about is only there because someone or something told you it was bad. The accuser of shame will always tempt you to blame. In the battle for your soul, blame will always point you away from the real enemy. We have to remember our fight isn't with each other. There is a real enemy. Ephesians 6:12 says, "For our struggle is not against flesh and blood, but against the rulers, against the authorities, against the powers of this dark world and against the spiritual forces of evil in the heavenly realms" (NIV).

> One of the scariest things I see in our culture today is the dangerous elimination of shame.

Shame coated with the cloak of accusation is not from the Holy Spirit. Conviction from God will always come with compassion. Compassion that feels like kindness. It will feel like the father of the prodigal son running out to meet the child he loves. It will feel like freedom, rescue, redemption. It will feel like someone gently taking the shame gun from you instead of pressing it down harder into your temple.

Unprocessed shame will always become fertile ground for evil to take root. The strategy of evil is to keep me from dealing with my silenced shame. A win for darkness is to keep me trapped under the shame gun with my finger always on the trigger. Getting to the root, the bottom, and the beginning of shame will be the hardest battle, but our greatest weapon against warfare.

When the rodent exterminator came to our house, he told us the very first thing to do to get rid of the rats was to take out the trash. Before setting traps or poison boxes, take out the trash. Where there is trash, the rats will come. Rats linger in the darkness of our leftovers. Like my dreadful root canal, the very source of my pain had to be destroyed or infection would manifest. We have to get to the seed of our shame.

Shame is always attached to a story. Something that happened to us, from us, because of us. It tells us we are bad. Our shame stories all started somewhere. Maybe it was in a locked room, a school hallway, an email with an image. Maybe it was when we saw our mother's pain, our father's disappointment, or our sibling's rage. Maybe it was a mistake we made, a car accident we caused, or a situation where we lost control.

In these stories we made an agreement. It may not have been a written or even verbal contract, but an agreement was made. Like a whisper in our soul, we made a vow. *I am too sensitive. I am responsible. I can't let people down. I must be needed. I have to have control. I must win. I can't show weakness. I am always dirty. I must keep the peace. I must hold everyone together. I have to protect. I can't make mistakes. I can't trust myself. If I don't do it, no one will. I must be quiet. I must be right. I am always dependable. If anyone ever finds out, people will be mad. People always leave. I must ease the tension with my goodness. It's my fault.* We made these promises to avoid pain, but in reality, they throw us deeper into it. These agreements that were shaped by our stories must be uprooted. These are the agreements where the demonic forces meddle with us the most.

We must re-enter these stories. We must rip back the rug we've swept unwanted things under. We can't avoid them, rewrite them, pretend that they don't exist. We can't let the power of shame propel us away from getting at the cracked foundation. We can't let the temptation to blame keep us from finding where the shame really stems from. We must go to the place where the vows were made and, with the authority we have been given, extract them.

Darkness only stays dark when there is no light. Rats only linger where there is trash. The moment we turn on the lights, the rats scatter. Light always reveals truth. Always. Jesus is the light of the world and has given us authority over evil. In the moments when our pain is triggered and we find ourselves instantly spiraling, suffocating, confused, furious, and drowning, we don't have to depend on our agreements anymore. It's so scary to break them. Terrifying, really. These promises have falsely made us feel safe and secure. God has given me power over the demonic. He has given me authority to fight the forces of darkness in the world and inside of myself. In the name of Jesus, I have all authority in heaven and on earth. The power isn't in me, it is through Jesus.

Jesus, who heals the sick. Jesus, who sees the poor, broken, lost, and lonely. Jesus, who loves the outcast and the righteous. Jesus, who shows compassion on the adulterous woman and tax collector. Jesus, who touches the man with leprosy. Jesus, who cast out demons into a herd of pigs. Jesus, who raises the dead.

Jesus, who calms the storm and controls the wind. Through the very name of Jesus, I have authority over darkness, over ugliness, over evil. In that place where I feel unbearably stuck—there is a way out. For the relationship that I've stopped believing could ever change—redemption is possible. When I speak the name of Jesus into the agreements I've made—freedom comes. It might not come that exact moment, but when my heart engages in the real battle with the real power against evil, victory will come. This is not the end. Jesus has the final say.

When shame holds a gun to my head, I speak "Jesus."

When a poisonous, evil, nasty thought pops into my mind in the middle of a nice afternoon, "Jesus."

When I crumble under the weight of carrying the world, "I break the agreement I've made to hold all the responsibility—in Jesus' name."

When I can't please everyone, "I break the vow I've made to never disappoint anyone—in Jesus' name."

When I spiral because I was accused of being wrong, "I break the vow I've made to be perfect—in Jesus' name."

When someone is angry, upset, or distant and I start to scramble, "In Jesus' name—I smash the agreement I've made to assume I am always at fault for their pain."

Every single agreement I've made in the darkness must come to the light. I can face evil because the love of God greets me with all compassion the same way He met the woman at the well, with no condemnation, only kindness. Once the root of my pain has been destroyed, pain will cease just like my horrible, rotten, no-good tooth.

Wake up, sister. I know you have secret thoughts that haunt you. I know shame still lingers in the dark corners of your soul. Pay attention to the places in your life where you are stuck. Where are you choking? When does your body go cold? Pay attention to where and when you start to feel out of control and let it be an indictor to you that evil is at play. What shame holds you hostage? What agreements have you made since you were young? What voices mock you? What whispers do you hear in the night? Wake up to the evil pain controlling you. You know what it feels like. It is snake-like, slow, and strikes hard. You are a daughter of the King. No evil can harm you. No scheme can destroy you. No secret can kill you.

You, sister, have wrestled with shame your entire life. But wake up. God has given you power to overcome the evil one. You don't have to put yourself in prison any longer. The name of Jesus sets you free. Wake up and out of the slumber of spiritual darkness blinding you. Wake up. Don't be deceived into believing that blackness is actually brightness. If there is a gun pointing at you, you are asleep to the light of Christ. Jesus already took the bullets. Jesus took the gun. Jesus took evil on and defeated it. Reclaim your birthright. Announce the authority you have been given. No darkness, no fear, no demonic powers, no shame, no person, place, or thing can ever rip you away from the love of God.

In all these things we are more than conquerors through him who loved us. For I am sure that neither death nor life, nor angels nor rulers, nor things present nor things to come, nor powers, nor height nor depth, nor anything else in all creation,

will be able to separate us from the love of God in Christ Jesus
our Lord.

Romans 8:37–39

We eventually moved back into our rodent-infested house. It took months to get rid of the rats. All the walls went up and holes were filled in. We took out the trash every night. Sam stayed up one evening and hunted the evil creatures with a broom. We even got a cat that my children love and I desperately try to like.

Our home went under reconstruction, but so did I. When my walls were opened, I saw dark forces lingering in the shadows. I had let trash build up. I gave all my energy to maintaining my quiet agreements. I believed if I kept these promises, I would be loved. I was consumed by the commitments I made in the dark.

When I stay and pay attention to my inner agreements, only then can I be awake to the authority I have in Christ. Only then does the darkness loosen its grip on me. The demonic realm has no real power over my soul.

In the end, rats are just rats. They are skittish and not all that smart. Darkness is not the end of the story. The sun is always itching to rise. The end comes when my foundation has been built on the love of God alone. Not by my power to hold up my end of a bargain. Only when I stand on the authority I have in Christ does darkness cease being dark.

12

Debbie from the Plane

Wake up to more joy

Debbie from the plane," her name caught my attention as I was going through the contacts on my phone. Debbie! I closed my eyes. I could see her bouncy hair matching her boisterous southern drawl. Instantly, I was transported back to that June day when I met Debbie. It was the day my plane almost crashed. I boarded the plane headed from San Diego to Denver on a cool morning. It was a trip I was hesitant to take. I was on my way to a retreat. For over a year, I had been a contributing writer to a blog called (in)courage with a few dozen other Christian writers. I had known a few of these women from online, but they weren't necessarily my friends. I'd rather spend my weekends with my kids and my husband, and in my own bed. If I could take my mattress, linens, and pillow with me, I'd travel anywhere. But leaving them home felt exhausting. Meeting new people didn't sound relaxing. It felt like work. But I packed up my bags, kissed my baby goodbye, and dragged my sluggish body onto the plane with a book, my phone, and an anxious spirit.

I don't like flying. Since 9/11 I'd rather take a bus. I avoid bridges, high buildings, and small, enclosed areas. My mind looks like hangers tangled up on a closet floor when I'm in a cramped space. I get a little anxious. My chest feels like it's in a straitjacket, and my breathing turns into a quick pant. As luck would have it, I had the middle seat. "Just breathe," I told myself. The gal beside me, Lynn, was clearly an extrovert. I didn't mind her chattiness. Her stories took my mind off all the what-ifs I could masterfully come up with.

Our casual conversation started at 10:18 when the plane took off and was interrupted by the turmoil at around noon. The two-hour flight was nearing its end when the bumps began. Our seatbelts were secure, seat backs upright, carry-on baggage tucked away, and tables pinned closed. As the plane approached the landing strip, it bobbled back and forth like a ping-pong ball in the hands of a two-year-old. The pilot immediately pulled the plane straight up like a rocket launching into space. My hands clenched the seat divider. The sound of the engine surged so loudly it covered the screams. I texted Sam and asked him to pray. The pilot said something about air pockets, the storm, and how everything was going to be okay. Out the window everything was murky; the clouds were as dark and thick as molasses. The plane circled for another ten minutes before the pilot attempted another landing. This time I grabbed Lynn's hand. She didn't resist. I thought about my family. I thought about my babies. I prayed. I closed my eyes and found a safe place, a childlike place. My memory took me to a time I felt Jesus. I remember the sky was black and the stars were putting on a light show just for me. This is probably the place where my deepest trust lives. It's a tender place and one of the first times I believed God was really real. It's this soft memory I held on to tightly as we tried to descend into Denver.

The front tires nearly touched the gravel before an air pocket bounced the back end of the plane up and out of control. I could actually feel the pilot trying to regain control of the plane, like a race car driver who took a turn way too fast. Then, like Hawkeye's arrow, the plane shot back into the sky with a force. Unsuccessfully the pilot attempted one more dangerous landing before we were rerouted to Grand Junction Airport, an hour away.

When our plane finally landed, every passenger belted out a hearty cheer. I texted Sam and hugged Lynn, my new best friend. Before I could even unbuckle, the pilot informed us we had to wait. We had to wait for a new crew and a new plane. So, we waited. Fifteen minutes, thirty minutes, and then an hour. We were getting restless. The plane wasn't stocked with food, and water was limited. Nothing good happens when angry, hot, cramped, starved, and scared survivors of an almost plane crash are trapped for any amount of time in a tiny space.

Panic only increased when the pilot came over the loud-speaker and said buses were coming to pick everyone up to drive us back to Denver. Buses! Lynn, a Colorado local, mouthed at me, "That's going to take hours by bus!" We grabbed our things and nicely shoved our way off the plane. I knew this nice shove. Anyone who has ever waited in a line to get into a concert, a packed theater, or a live sports event knows this nice shove. You smile and nod, but never make eye contact. You don't let an inch of space bubble up between you and the person in front of you. You can't make room for anyone to get to the on-ramp of the freeway that leads to the thing you really want. I have the nice shove down.

When we finally got off that dreaded plane, Lynn and I ran toward the rental cars. I should rather say, it looked like a clumsy jog. We were two middle-aged women trying to run with our carry-ons, phones in one hand and dragging luggage on wheels behind us. It was awkward and certainly uncomfortable to watch. It wasn't a pretty run. Unfortunately, we weren't the only ones who had this genius idea, but we joined the race anyway. The air was hot from the heat storm, my stomach rumbling with hunger, and my fighter instinct kicked in strong. I sprinted faster. I would not take a bus. I would not stay the night in a dingy motel. I would not be outrun by the college kid who could easily hitchhike and risk death by a stranger. Two hundred desperate passengers hurried toward the Avis, Enterprise, and Hertz counters. This tiny commuter airport had never seen so much business. The lines were Disneyland long by the time Lynn and I got there. We waited. We tried to outsmart people and reserve a car online with our smartphones. No luck. We got to the front. All the cars were gone.

I was gathering my courage to ride a bus back to Denver when the rental car guy said, "I do have one twelve-passenger van." He dangled the keys. A tantalizing idea tickled me. I looked at Lynn and the Asian couple with the baby behind us. To my left was a family of four. I started doing the math. Yes! We can do this. It might just work. I gathered the closest strangers in a huddle like we were planning out our next strategic play. In a wild turn of events, we almost felt giddy. Twelve strangers from around the country, meeting for the first time, overcoming a near-death experience, were now traveling together in a van with one destination in mind—Denver.

> Like embers glow after a fire dies, my dreams held on as long as possible, until the light was completely gone.

I'm not sure I'd ever been on a detour quite like this one before. I've lived a rather predictable life. I'd gone the school-marriage-house-kids-and-a-cat route. When I was younger, I dreamed big dreams. I wouldn't be like everyone else. I'd live differently. I'd travel, move far away, eat food I couldn't pronounce, and pursue the highest levels of education. Yet, I live in the same town I grew up in and drive an SUV. I haven't swerved off the path very far. Somehow, I always come back to the rattle and hum of normal—pack-the-lunches, plan-the-birthday-party, what's-for-dinner life. In the middle of motherhood and household responsibilities and remembering to cancel the doctor's appointment, my mind sometimes wanders to the life I dreamed of living after college.

After having babies, I thought I would just put those dreams "on hold." For a long time, I actually said that phrase, "put on hold." I think a part of me believed I would go back to my life before kids one day. The life where I could jump in a car and go on a road trip, and the hardest thing to decide was what movie to watch at the theater. When my kids could walk or were out of the house, I could get back to "that life." But I didn't realize that I wasn't putting my life "on hold." I had to put that life to death. I don't mean I tossed myself aside like an old diaper and became a doormat. I mean I had to make a conscious choice to put the needs of my kids before mine. Dying to my dreams was painful. Dying to life moving on my timeline was aggravating. It hurt everything—body, soul, ego. My plans weren't put "on hold" but had to be held openly. The fists that held all my desires now held babies, wipes, and an extra change of clothes for the inevitable blowout. My life before babies had to be grieved. Like embers glow after a fire dies, my dreams held on as long as possible, until the light was completely gone. God was growing a new dream.

My mom was a stay-at-home mom even though she had a PhD. She could have had a job at any university in America. She set aside her career, money, and accolades to be the snack mom for my class. She held me after every nap, let me sit on the counter while she made lunches, and had me "help" her fold laundry. For me, for now, staying home was what felt right. I wanted to be the one rocking my babies to sleep. Sometimes it was glorious, while other times I cried because it was so hard to put aside life on my terms. I felt lost, alone, ashamed, angry, and some days just plain bored. I couldn't tell anyone how desperate I felt. I couldn't explain how I *did* want to be home with my kids, but something inside of me also felt smothered.

Perhaps this is the pain of the dying. The ache, pull, twist, and exhale of letting go and moving forward. This raw, "I want to cry all the time" sting was the irritating twinge of letting go and learning what it meant to sacrifice. I knew I would never regret this decision, but I also knew it was costing me everything. Walking forward into the unknown felt like a saltless dish. It felt blah. Every day thoughts would shimmy through my mind: What was I doing with my life? What was I doing with my master's degree and the loan payment I was resentfully making every month? Here I was pouring orange juice, preparing meals on tiny plates, cutting off unwanted crust, and driving kids to preschool.

During nap time and between loading dishes, I jotted down my chaotic thoughts. I propped open my laptop after bedtime. With my wild sweet orange tea and the glow of a screen, I'd type my anxious feelings. After several months, I printed out what, to my surprise, seemed to be a book. I held all my stories, from breaking to being reborn, between my palms. Then, I placed them in our office desk along with my diploma. Instead of chasing my dreams, I put them in a drawer.

Sacrifice can often get confused with submission. Somehow sacrifice can turn into this idea that I'm not standing up for myself, or I must silence my voice. It can seem weak, passive, or less than. But sacrifice is the soul discipline of moving from "my will be done" to "thy will be done." Sacrifice isn't suppression. It isn't just an outward action. It is an internal, unseen, slow growing work of the Spirit that takes me from getting to giving, striving to serving, and pursuing to pausing. Sacrifice is the action that puts into motion the transformation of life on my terms to a life lived on God's terms.

Sacrifice is the release of my gifts, abilities, needs, desires, time, power, and feelings—to put another's gifts, abilities, needs, desires, time, power, and feelings before mine. It doesn't mean what I want doesn't matter. It means I am making a choice to let others go first. Like opening a door and holding it for another to walk in. But in my case, the door is a heavy steel one and the people going through it are my children. Instead of moving along nicely through the passageway like normal human beings, they are revolting against common sense by licking the ground and swinging like baboons from the door frame. If you can't find me, I'll be hiding in my closet with sour candy and a liter of Coke for a few years while I recover. It feels tedious, thankless, and tiring. I can't tell you how many times I sat in my parked car and cried under the weight of motherhood.

> Sacrifice is the action that puts into motion the transformation of life on my terms to a life lived on God's terms.

Sacrifice is for the good of others, but also for me. For me, in this season of my life, sacrifice meant starting a journey of dying to the past and walking into a dry season of drawing baths and checking homework. It felt like a detour and like I was on a mapless journey. Yet, between the hard moments, the sky would part and heaven would shine out its happy face. I saw it in the eyes of my children learning to read their name for the first time. I saw it when they celebrated flipping a pancake or successfully folding a paper airplane. In the midst of grieving my old life and embracing my new one, even in the breaking, I saw joy. I felt it. I found pops of color coming at me like driving on the freeway and seeing neon graffiti grabbing my attention in unexpected delight. In a way I couldn't see yet, I was becoming the person I needed to be. A person pulled apart and put back together through the day-in, day-out, painful, slow-changing work of sacrifice. An unseen layer of selfishness was being cracked inside of me. A selfishness I hadn't seen inside of me before was being unleashed. I saw my ugly. I saw my sin. I saw how desperate I was to have things go my way all the time. Daily, unseen, sacrificial acts done as a mom were the very ways God was teaching me to love, a selfless, giving, "I'll hold the dense door even if it's hard for me" kind of love.

What I see now is that God was nurturing me in this new season. He was transforming my "I'll do it my way" to a way of humility. Through this detour God was teaching me how to consider others better than myself (Philippians 2:3). I see how all the mundane, unnoticeable, tiring mornings meant I was becoming a woman who could love well. When I screamed—I was learning my limits. When I wanted to run away, but didn't—I was learning faithfulness. When I felt defeated by the nonstop needs—I was learning dependence on Christ. When Sam was home late from work and a disagreement erupted—I was learning to forgive and ask for forgiveness.

Sacrifice wasn't a detour; it was the way God was teaching me how to love from a pure heart. He revealed my heart and my temptation to seek praise. He showed me my selfishness. He unclasped my brass heart fastened together by the compliments of others and replaced them with beads on a rosary— each moment an act of trusting Him. This detour cost me the life I thought I wanted. It cost me my reputation, money in my bank account, and career advancement. But in exchange, I gained everything. I gained joy. Oh, I also gained amazing relationships with my kids, who are no longer wild baboons and, from time to time, hold the door for me now.

Nine adults, two children, and one baby elbowed each other into a twelve-seater van. The road trip would take most of the day. That's when I met Debbie. "Debbie from the plane" sat right next to me. She was sassy, blunt, and full of quick, say-what-everyone's-really-thinking-but-too-afraid-to-say-out-loud comebacks. Her husband reminded me of Jack from *Lost* and instantly became the leader of our new-formed tribe. He drove the van all the way from Grand Junction to Denver. This small group of strangers bonded. We shared Goldfish crackers, told stories, and used each other's phone chargers. We played a question game called Would You Rather? for a solid two hours. We passed around family photos. Debbie's two elementary aged daughters drilled us with questions. We all laughed so hard. My heart expanded like those magical foam mattresses you get in the mail. I grew to really enjoy these people.

On the drive Debbie told me about her faith and how disheartened she was by the church. I didn't offer answers, but I listened. She shared about how her grandfather was a preacher and how she wants to raise kind children. I reminded her of how God never loses sight of us no matter how broken life gets. I shared my Jesus journey too.

We all have a story, don't we? Every stranger, every human, every soul has a story. I got to hear Debbie's. And in the most unimaginable way, with the gray sun dropping behind the storm-covered Colorado mountains, I smiled. This journey that ended up taking me a total of sixteen hours was what my soul needed. I needed to be stuck in a van with strangers to see people again. I needed a hand to hold when death burned in me like a jet engine. I needed to remember how fragile life really is. I needed to listen, laugh, and connect on a human level with people who were in many ways just like me. I could have driven from San Diego to Denver in less time than this massive detour took me. But in some unbelievable way, I wouldn't change it. God always knows what we need. He will take us on the long route if it means He can give us the water our souls are really longing for.

Our souls are hungry. Each soul has an ache, hurt, longings, and quiet discontentment. When what we crave can't be claimed by the tactics we use, we can get desperate. We can become people we don't want to be. We can get controlling, demanding, blinded, irritated, and irate. We wonder why we aren't the people we want to be. We lose sight of all the good we actually have. God will starve us off the strategies we use to meet our souls' needs apart from Him. He is always weaning us from a life of autonomy to a life of love, from *my* will to *thy* will.

God will take us on a journey, one we may never have chosen, to reconstruct our hidden hearts into holy love.

Wake up, sister. I know you have desires. I know your soul is hungry. Feel your hunger right now. Is it in your stomach, thoughts, throat, or spirit? Touch your head, heart, and gut. You might even be in a place where you feel like your desires have been forgotten. The path you are on might not make logical sense. Perhaps the place you are in life isn't where you thought you'd be. When you look at your current circumstances, you may feel behind or off track from your plan. The temptation will be to look at your life like it's a calculus problem to solve. Resist this. Instead, enter your life. Be where God has led you. Stay where He has invited you to

> God will starve us off the strategies we use to meet our souls' needs apart from Him.

be. Let your body, mind, and heart all be in the same place. Be fully in it even when it feels muddled, uncomfortable, and incredibly confusing.

Love is hard. Sacrifice is hard. If it's hard you aren't doing something wrong, you are walking the narrow road of sacrifice. Trust in God. Lean on Him with all your strength, all your hopes, and all your capacities. Don't, for a second, believe God has lost sight of you. Don't allow discomfort or a fantasy to determine your exit strategy when circumstances are trying. The Spirit will lead you with wisdom when it's time to move on. Until then, wake up. Take note of the space you hold in the world. It is more beautiful because you are in it. Let it be here that you pour out all your devotion. Let it be here that you fully invest your gifts, time, love, and untamed imagination.

As you fully give yourself to the "detours" in life, you'll start to discover unexpected joy. Sister, more and more joy will emerge. Joy won't come because your circumstances change, but because you are present to the life God has gifted to you. Where you once saw dread, you will begin to see blessings welcoming you in like the coziest chunky blanket draping from the couch onto the floor. Sister, listen for the nudges, talk to the stranger, take the scenic route, slow down instead of speeding up, wait for the next elevator, look up from your phone. God's divine detour is leading you into deeper trust with Him. He is making space for more connection. God uses all things for His good. Every. Single. Thing. It's what God does. He uses circumstances to draw out our impurities and draw us closer to Him. He uses the story you are walking in today, right now, to fulfill the story He has always been writing. Don't miss the joy because you are so focused on the future. Sister, wake up and receive the detours as divine invitations to the greatest, deep down soul smiles.

Jesus was always headed to Jerusalem. He was always making His way to the cross. The path was a zigzag. He followed the cries of the wounded requesting healing. He went out of His way to care for the hurting. He purposefully went toward the woman at the well even though it meant walking miles off the target destination. He stayed longer when people asked him to. Jesus was always taking detours to meet His children. It doesn't make sense; it looks backwards and wasteful. Our world tells us if we want to get ahead, we have to hurry up. If we want to live life to the fullest, we have to push harder. If we want to succeed, we have to have a side hustle. But Jesus says if you want more you need to become less. If you want true life, you have to sacrifice. In this way of living, nothing is ever lost. No sacrifice is returned empty. The blind see; the children are seen; the wine is replenished. Every detour, every sacrifice, every this-doesn't-make-sense situation comes with joy because Christ is close. Sometimes it's physical, and sometimes it's metaphorical, but every time if we stay awake to God's story within our own, we will find resurrection. On the way to resurrection your story will loop, turn, twist, and idle in neutral. Parts of you will die, but the Spirit is always slowly tapping your soul to wake up. Rising will come.

New rising came for my mom when after twenty years of staying at home raising kids, she got a job teaching English at Point Loma Nazarene University. This would be the same school I would attend with two of my sisters. Because of her full-time position, our education was completely paid for. In the end, her dusty PhD saved us over $150,000. Rising came. Seven years after I printed out my story on recycled computer paper, it was published and sold on shelves around the world. Rising came. Detours are never the end of the story.

I'm not saying when we sacrifice, we get everything we want. I'm saying that when we sacrifice, we get to see God giving us things we never deserved in the first place. We get the undeserved gift of joy along the journey. Detours, if followed, can lead to beautiful miracles. But nothing has been more beautiful than to see what the Spirit did inside of me when it seemed like He was doing nothing at all. In the middle, I felt forgotten, unseen, and depleted. But in the middle there was also joy. Through sacrifice, layers and layers were shed, layers that clogged my ability to love. Layers that strapped my soul down like a tight seatbelt. But the middle is where God did the most

> I'm not saying when we sacrifice, we get everything we want. I'm saying that when we sacrifice, we get to see God giving us things we never deserved in the first place.

work. In the dark when it was hard to see, God was doing the most radical reconstruction. The detour wasn't a detour at all.

I arrived at the (in)courage retreat at two in the morning. When I pulled into the hotel, a deer skipped by me. This wasn't San Diego anymore. I was among wildlife. I was exhausted, but I still couldn't sleep. It smelled like Christmas outside, and the pine trees reached as high as the stars, so it seemed. Everything

felt fresh. I could breathe. I closed my eyes and remembered my day. I thought about the plane and how when I was confronted with death, my mind went to the tenderest place inside of me. I went to Jesus, my joy. I went to that evening when I looked out my second-story window and saw Jesus through the night sky. He was loving me then like He was loving me now through the Colorado mountain air and stars, mesmerizing my soul by His love song in space.

When we feel lost, Jesus meets us in our most delicate places and draws us to himself. Even in my compassless days, Jesus is leading me by the way of sacrifice. He is leading me like the wise men to new life. The detours are not indicators of my progress or failures, but evidence of the One I am following. I am led by love. Even in the unknown I can trust that pure love is purifying me. Even in the most grimacing story, God is persistent to grow me. Even in the darkest winter, nothing can stop the spring. If the place you find yourself isn't promising, look beyond and beneath what you can tangibly see. Trust that the character of Christ is reconstructing your character for greater good. He will use all things to make beautiful new things in you. A new season is just around the bend.

I wondered if I would ever see Lynn, the sweet Asian family, or Debbie again. I wondered what everything meant. I'm not sure I will ever know why things happened the way they did, but I do know that tucked into this tumultuous day were moments popping with joy. I do know that at the end of my life I want my phone filled with contacts that say things like "Mike the guy from the grocery store" and "Alice the gal who served us breakfast" and "Debbie from the plane." I want to know I followed the detours, the long, arduous, dying-to-dreams, talking-to-strangers kinds of detours—because sacrifice in every shape leads to an awakening of God's love story inside of mine.

13

It Was the Perfect Day

Wake up to more power

t was the perfect day. It began by waking up in cold sheets in a soothingly warm room. Before opening my eyes, I could smell summer. I love the shift from spring to summer, a subtle and almost unnoticeable change in San Diego. But natives to this desert wonderland can sense it. We feel it. The humidity moves in quietly like the sun across a sapphire sky. You never know the moment evening begins; it just arrives and lasts long.

Summer settles in like a balmy breeze with the orange blossoms in sad denial that their show is coming to a close. I grieve a bit too, because year after year, the way they burst off the trees in fragrance and florals is a performance that certainly deserves an encore. That's what summer does, it ushers in more and more radiant, shimmering, bright—beauty.

Summer was near. Summer with its cool mornings, muggy hot days, and late-setting sun had come. Summer with its laid-back, windows-down, play-all-day attitude, chlorine-green hair, dyed Otter Pops, and happy-hungry mosquitoes had arrived. The morning of my perfect day the most gleeful hydrangeas greeted me on the clean counters. Flowers elegant, white, and heavenly leaned slant in a mason jar next to my sink. Hydrangeas are like lace to me. They add almost unnoticeable loveliness to everything. Like lace lining the edge of a blouse, linen, or tablecloth, they add just a touch of specialness. Delicate lace isn't a detail that demands attention. It isn't even necessary, for that matter. It is as soft and as tender as a half-smile. Like lace, my white hydrangeas were simple, gentle, and secure enough to barely reflect off my shiny counters. Cornerless like clouds, the soft petals stood effortlessly on the surface like puffed sleeves on a Sunday dress.

I poured water into my orange tea kettle and waited for the whistle. The morning light was as expectant and as yellow as freshly cut lemons. My tea was brewing. My heart was swelling. Everything was perfect.

I wouldn't consider myself a perfectionist in the classical sense. I don't need the apps on my screen color coordinated or all the shoes straight. If the dishwasher can close, that's good enough for me. We have about eight junk drawers, and the scissors can be found in a dozen different places. This doesn't bother me. I am hardly ever on time. I don't like to use blue tape when I paint walls. I squeeze my toothpaste tube in the middle. I go by the "about" system. I'll be there at *about* noon, add *about* a cup of sugar, that's *about* right. I don't need to be perfect, but there are different kinds of perfectionists.

I need to be perfect for others. I need experiences to be perfect. I need to have control. Sometimes I think I have a sixth sense of perceiving the feelings of people and the mood in a room. Call it intuition. I can walk into a sanctuary, grocery store, or dentist's office and just know the emotions in the space. I can read people and the room like I can paint by numbers; it's so easy. I can pick up on body language instantly. I can feel out the lonely people and the powerful ones. I can sniff out the fake ones too. The anxious people are the easiest to spot. I can feel people's feelings as if they were my own. I sense them, see them, and absorb them like a sponge.

If I could control the environment, I could control the emotions. If I made the right kind of eye contact, asked the right questions, or listened the right way, I could control the outcome. It was my superpower. I had to use it for everything to be perfect. In fact, I must use it.

Many "musts" dictate my life. I call these my ten commandments. Thou shalt not make people unhappy. Thou shalt not upset people. Thou shalt have control. Thou shalt not be imperfect. If I break these commandments, something inside of me breaks. This doesn't always bring out the most flattering sides of my personality. I can be snippy and passive aggressive and stubborn. I can be angry and eye-rolly and anxious. I can turn into a wide-eyed, chewing-my-fingernails-off crazy person. My wedding was so stressful because of my neurotic "thou shalt nots." It was scary. My perfectionist tendency is a strong, almost desperate need to secure everything on the outside, so everything on the inside of me feels powerful.

This perfect day with summer's arrival and the hydrangeas as pretty as puffed sleeves was just another day I carried everyone's emotions. We swam and devoured watermelon. The kids didn't scream at each other once. The ceiling outside was expansive, blue, and cloudless, like a swimming pool in the sky. I sat in the shade with my soda and chewable ice. I biasly judged the kids' diving competition (the youngest in the family always wins). For dinner we drizzled Sam's homemade barbecue sauce over tri-tip, sprinkled salt and lime zest onto crisp grilled corn, and deep fried french fries. Drinking slow sips of agua fresca, we sat under the twinkling lights and the girls danced.

Nothing is better than a summer evening. The gentle warmth, light breeze, and sun that never seems to set allow the day to go on forever. We roasted marshmallows to a perfect rust hue, spread creamy Nutella across graham crackers, and consumed sweetness until the stars came out. While the boys found things to burn in the firepit, the girls brought out every one of their stuffed animals, pillows, and blankets. They created an observatory to watch the stars from our back deck. On our backs we stargazed, tracing the constellations with our fingertips.

These perfect moments are the ones I want mapping out the rest of my life. It's moments like these that roll out the future I want like a red carpet. I've always wanted a large family. I want all the noise and a million shoes lining the entryway. I want the chaos. I want the big car and the Costco runs that drain the bank account but fill up our bodies. I want a lot of young and old people seated around our outdoor table one day. I want elbows overlapping, forks scraping, and eight different conversations happening all at once. I want laughter erupting like contagious pops of happiness from one end of the table to the other. This perfect day was a taste of what I hoped would continue on decades into the future. I could always see it in my imagination, but today, I held a pocket-sized glimpse of what I hoped would come. Everyone is close and connected. Everything perfect. And as I lay, shoulder to shoulder, with Noelle watching the stars dance across the dark, I felt a tightening in my stomach as she spoke.

She asked me if I had been to the stars. Had I gone to the moon or space? I smiled. Without waiting for my answer, she listed all the places she would go one day: New York, Seattle, Spain, Greek (she meant Greece), and the Middle East. She wanted to go where the stars shine brightest. Though I've always known my kids would grow up, I never really imagined them leaving. A painful pulling started to take place inside my soul. My perfect day, tearing. I'm not ready to turn in tutus for tampons. I refuse to put away the Legos and turn on the porch light. I don't want my babies to become big. I want to braid baby hair and hear the giggles from the other room. I want the anticipation of wiggly teeth and noses pressed flat against the glass at the ice cream shop. I want to freeze time at these ages and keep them safe right here forever. How is it possible that one day they won't need me to buckle them in, tuck them under blankets, and hold them even when the scary part is over? I am exiting the baby years of motherhood, and I don't know how to do it. I don't know how to let go. All I feel is my heart ripping open as my little girl dreams about touching the stars. Right here, right now, with her right beside me, I still have control.

Even on my most perfect day, perfect isn't enough. The perfect now and perfect dream of someday will leave me with more longings. I can't hold on to my kids. I can't stop them from walking out my front door and never coming home. I can't keep my girl with her fine blond hair and dimpled chin from being rejected or falling for a boy who won't love her back. I can't change the outcome. I can't make my boys into fine young men or keep them from one computer click that could destroy their lives. My kids aren't vending machines. I can't deposit time, energy, and love and expect a certain outcome. I can deposit all of me into their slow-growing souls, and they might still turn their backs on each other, Jesus, or what I think is best for them.

Probably the most terrifying Bible passage for me is Luke 14:26: "If anyone comes to me and does not hate his own father and mother and wife and children and brothers and sisters, yes, and even his own life, he cannot be my disciple." I usually casually skip over the passage. I don't like it. Although I don't think Jesus is saying to hate people in your life, I think it pings a deep place of pain in my heart that I'd rather not feel. I think what Jesus means here is don't cling to people to give you life. Don't cling to your parents for approval, don't depend on your siblings to give you praise, don't rest on your children to resolve your loneliness. Love people, but don't let these relationships become your drug to substitute for God's love.

Perhaps Jesus knows how fragile my human heart is, how I tend to consume others in order to heal the deep wounds inside of me. He knows my impossible need to make sure everyone's emotions are cared for. He knows how desperately I want to feel safe, good, and okay. He knows I will do whatever it takes to control external space for my internal peace. He knows my temptation to strap people on my back and just *make* relationships work no matter how toxic they are. Jesus knew I would consume people like they were my oxygen. But Jesus says, "hate." The invitation is to hate. The invitation is to break. It is to not just break this law in my heart, but to hate it. Hate the way I need to be needed, hate my superpower to save, hate what I think a perfect life looks like. Don't hate the people, but hate the dysfunctional ways I relate to them. My "thou shalt nots" need to be broken if I am ever going to live. If I don't hate the laws I've created for myself, I will suffocate.

> My "thou shalt nots" need to be broken if I am ever going to live.

When I was a child, I frequently visited my family in Thailand. My extended family was Buddhist. My grandpa was orphaned as a baby and left on the steps of a monastery. He was raised by monks, who became like big brothers and fathers. In the humid summers, I'd play with my sisters and the street kids on the dusty back roads of Chiang Mai, Thailand. We'd play tag and jump rope and soccer with deflated balls. We'd communicate rules through the universal language of hand motions and laughter and drawing stick figures in dirt. When the heat was unbearable, we scavenged for coins under cushions and chased down street carts for ice cream and frozen sugar pops. The gross heat and annoying mosquitoes were miserable most days.

Inside, I scampered up the narrow, rickety bamboo staircase, my sticky bare feet smacking the hardwood floors. A side room was always off-limits. A sheer curtain hung loosely up on a rod. I smelled potent incense before I could see anyone inside. I moved in closer, my eyes nervously surveying the mystery behind the cloth divider and strong scent. My grandpa was on his knees with candles glowing and slender incense sticks burning smoke up to the ceiling; I saw an aged version of my dad bowing down to a statue of Buddha. The room was smoky and dark and eerie. I saw him come up and down, nose to knees, hands pressed together from face to floor. I was so nervous to be seen. I was a skinny girl, sneaking to see what kind of magic was happening between my grandpa and that gold figure with a big round belly. My grandfather was bending over before a shiny image that he bought at the market. I was so curious and confused. It made me feel a little afraid, but very much intrigued. I avoided that room, but I was always aware of its uncomfortable presence, like a guest at a party sitting alone in the corner. But no matter where I was, scampering down back streets or falling asleep, I could always smell that scary room, as if the scent followed me.

It was so odd seeing a strong man bend over to a statue. But as I get older, I realize my idols aren't so different from my grandfather's. I don't buy my statues at the store, but I build them, brick by brick, inside of me. They've grown right up and out of my heart. Mine are man-made too. My ten commandments and my soul statues are my idols. I worship my idols. If I relate a certain way to the idols, I believe my idols will then give me something in return. It is a relational agreement.

If you could see my idols in physical form, there would be a statue of each one of my children, Sam, and my perfect life with lots of people plopped right onto a shelf like trophies. A statue representing each of my relationships, from parents to sisters to lifelong friendships. Statues of my house, the book I've written, and my master's degree. I'd have a statue of my career, my creativity, my accomplishments, the places I've traveled, what people think about me, who knows me. I'd have a statue of my skin color, wedding day, birth plan, motherhood, and my need to manage everyone's emotions. But the biggest statue, my gold one, would be me.

I worship all these statues. I want other people to worship them. I bow down. I have a ritual to make sure I appease them. I need to keep them happy, impressed, pleased, entertained, and propped up. I light my incense, close the curtain, and make secret promises. But these idols, my Anjuli-made statues—no matter how many times I bend over, sacrifice, love, and chant loud for—will never love me back. They will only and always demand that I do more. These "thou shalt nots" must be broken. These are the things I must hate because God knows they don't have breath enough to love me back. It is absolutely impossible for an idol to love me. Idols aren't real. They are plastic, imaginary, and store bought. They are an illusion. In the same way, the statues in that smoky room at my grandfather's house could never love him.

Like the rich young ruler in Matthew 19, I want eternal life. I present all the things I've done and do before God. I've kept all the commandments. I've been a good girl. But Jesus says if I want true life, I have to give up what I cling to for life. The choice is mine. I can walk away like the rich young ruler did, or I can break my idols to find true life. The only way these idols break is to hate them. If I'm honest, I don't think I've ever hated anyone before. Like really hated. I've disliked people strongly, but I don't think I've hated them. Hating is a death sentence.

But the truth is the lower I bow and the more I worship these idols, the more I am walking in death. It's my own hell. If you have walls lined with self-made statues, you know the death I speak of. You know how exhausting and painful and endless it is to keep all your idols appeased. When we go through life quietly chanting, "Please like me, love me, be okay with me, adore me, entertain me, see me, feed me, don't blame me, don't expose me, don't leave me, protect them, protect me, give me prosperity, give me power, give me health, give me youth, give me peace, give me safety, give me worth, tell me I'm good, tell me I'm perfect, give me children, give me pardon," it is like walking in death. The chanting can be subtle or screaming, but our idols will never be satisfied. We will only live in slavery. They will always demand more of us. The more we worship them, the more the need grows to worship them, the more we *must* worship them. So, we feed them and give them all of our thoughts, time, and affection because we are desperate for some version of the life we crave in return. We need our idols to affirm our goodness. This is the death of a soul.

Dying to the worship of these trophies we've elevated as gods is what Christ invites us to do. Die to this empty way of living. Smash the idols. Smash them the way Moses smashed the Ten Commandments. Smash them the way Jesus cleared the temple courtyard. Smash them the way Mary broke her bottle of nard at the feet of Jesus. Lying with my girls on the perfect day, Jesus was inviting me to smash my idol of the perfect life. Smash the idol I'd made of motherhood. Smash my need for control. There is almost a violence in the smashing. An obliteration. A force. A demolition.

The affection I've given away to my idols, I give back to God. He is the One who never breaks. No hatred could destroy Him. No death could defeat Him. God, in friendship, slipped into humanity with skin and skull and full of soul. From baby to boy to brother to broken body on a branch, Jesus is the only One who stands as a pure, holy statue, worthy of praise. He isn't lifeless, store bought, or easily bribed. He has a soul. He is constantly giving love back to us. We don't have to chant for it, beg for it, be good for it, or pay for it. We just have to do one thing. We have to hate those other statues, the ones who can never love us back, with strength and aggression and violence; we must break those statues. They have no power. Smash them like a glass at a Jewish wedding. Let it symbolize the breaking of one law in exchange for a new, irreversible love promise.

> Dying to the worship of these trophies we've elevated as gods is what Christ invites us to do.

So, I break my idols. I tear them down with power and force and conviction.

There is authority. I imagine it's the way I order my kids not to step into a busy street. I stand in front of them, eye level, without flinching, and say, "You will not go any further!" I draw a line. I make a boundary. The lies, the compulsive thoughts, the reckless stories that play on repeat must be retracted. When I hand over my power to other people, I must speak with the same kind of conviction. When I start to hate my idols, pain will certainly emerge. I'll have withdrawals. When the sting comes and the wound is stirred, I say these words: "You don't have the power to determine my worth." It can sound mean or insulting, but letting lies seep any deeper into my soul is unacceptable.

The fear is crippling. I don't know who I am if I'm not bowing to my idols. I don't know who I am without these attachments. Who am I if I'm not a good mom, good daughter, good person? Who am I if my friend is mad at me, my children make wrong choices, my motives are misunderstood, my dad is disappointed, my body grows two sizes, and all my efforts are useless? Who am I if I am a bad person? I bow lower and lower to my statues, trying to quiet my questions. I've convinced myself that if I just did a little bit more, the pain would stop. But I've spent my life doing more, and the ache throbs louder and longer. It keeps me up at night. I want freedom. Maybe the most important "must" is this one—I must give God back the power to determine who I am. God and God alone.

I won't worship my god of perfection. Smash. I won't carry the emotions of everyone else. Crash. I won't worship my god of family. Break. I won't worship my god of security. Destroyed. I shred my need to be a statue for anyone else too. I am powerless to gain or get affection. I am powerless to meet the needs of others. I am powerless to create a perfect life, marriage, culture, or future. I could bend, bow, beg, dance, do cartwheels, abuse, control, cut, cry, do back flips, and bleed, but I am completely powerless to control anything and anyone but me. I can, however, control who I adore. I can worship the idols or worship God. My temptation is to be propped up, praised, respected, needed, and significant to others. But this too is futile. I am not a statue. I am a human. Don't worship me, be with me. My identity, importance, and worth aren't found in being a good mom, wife, daughter, or friend, but in the One who calls me beloved.

My identity isn't in being a superhero, influencer, savior, or soul carrier, but in being a child of God. I belong to God. All the identities I have given away to other gods are recollected back to the only One who has the power to love me. For too many years I have given my power like a paintbrush to others to paint my worthiness. I have given people ample amounts of paint to make some sort of art in me. I need them to feel safe and seen. God is the only One who has proven himself worthy enough to paint my soul beautiful. He breathed me into being. I give God back the paintbrush. Only He can color me in. I imagine the color He paints my soul would be as orange as a sunset.

God doesn't use His power to push people down or prop himself up. We know the nature of God because we see the nature of Jesus. Jesus used His power to become powerless. He gave up His life to make a pathway for us to be beside Him. That is how God uses power. Power always becomes a pathway for love. He has the power to heal others, hold pain, make a home in me. He has the power to care for those I love and those I've lost. He has power to protect and save and secure everything that feels shaky in this world and inside of me. God has the power. He is safe enough to hold all the world steady.

When my idols are smashed, my soul has space for His love to stay. I want a soft soul. I want my soul to be open and pliable, the way peony petals relax when exposed to the sun. Power used in purity can be a means to love. I want to release and exhale and restore power to its rightful place. I want to offer love so honest and good that I am left overflowing instead of secretly expecting something in return. I want to see the strength in others as a gift, not a threat. I want a clean soul. One that isn't bound up in bowing down to get the favor of invisible gods. I want my sons and daughters to know a mother who sets them free to follow God's story in them, not a mom who loves with strings attached, suspicious eyes, and a controlling spirit.

> When my idols are smashed, my soul has space for His love to stay.

Wake up, sister. Cup your cheek with your hand for a moment. The softness you feel is the same softness of Christ. You don't have to be bound up inside. Christ can untangle your heart. Watch the movements of your soul. Watch the way your soul-eyes search for power. See how they scan the room, watch the innerweb, scroll, and seek more significance. Wake up to the ways you've built your tower of Babel. If you want to see your idols, ask yourself what would smash you if you didn't have it. What would break you if you didn't achieve it or get it? Would it crush you if you didn't look a certain way? Would it obliterate you if you didn't get that house, that position, that approval from a certain person? Would you be shattered if your mom didn't support you or a friend left you? If your boss was disappointed or people knew you didn't have a happy marriage, would you be completely undone? If someone heard you scream at your kids, didn't like you, knew you doubted your faith, saw your dirty car, didn't understand you, or questioned your good-ness, would you be able to sleep at night? Is there a person in your life that no matter what you do, it's never enough? Ask God to reveal the idols of your heart to you.

Sister, wake up to reality. The idols you've worshiped will never love you. Refuse to worship or give your heart to anything or anyone else but God. Stop begging bronze to love you back. Stop expecting it. Stop digging in volcanic rock hoping to find fresh water. Stop wasting your life. Smash the idols. When you don't know how to break the bondage these idols have over you, like a good Father, the Lord will break you away from them. In God's severe mercy, He will snip the ties that bind you to any other god but Him. Not in haste, but in love, God will bring you back to himself. You will always be given a choice. Like the rich young ruler, you can stay with Christ or stay with your idols (Mark 10:17–31). I hope you choose Jesus.

Wake up to the true power that comes when you are empow-ered only by the love of God. This kind of power will look like generosity instead of greed, freedom instead of fear, creativity instead of control, and joy instead of jealousy. It's the kind of power that will look like a pure heart. Stay awake to this kind of life-changing, soul-filling power, sister.

On this perfect day with the morning light and summer breeze I felt my body release. I knew the only way to real power was to surrender my story to Jesus. I smashed my idol of controlling my children and my children's stories as well. The day with the fire crackling like poppers at a surprise party, laughter contagious, and sun that never seems to set. This perfect day when my daughter dreamed of moving far, far away, I leaned in close. I felt her breath on my face. I let my heart quietly ooze with grief. My goodness, she's beautiful. I'm tempted to worship her. I'm tempted to let her worship me and to become her idol, propped up, shiny and strong. She is my first daughter. My little idol I've birthed, nursed, raised, and rocked to sleep. I'm tempted to stuff her right into my heart, so I feel safe. I hold her cheeks. I cup her sweet face in my hands and look hard into her hazel eyes and with an unwavering whisper I say, "Follow God wherever He takes you, Noelle. Go to your *Greek* and faraway places. Go see the stars." And right there on the back deck I felt my Noelle idol smash in my soul. I set her free.

It was the perfect day. Perfection came in the light like thinly sliced lemons across my counter. It came through accepting my powerlessness and waking up to God, the One who is all powerful. His power doesn't demand my perfection or chanting or soul smashing. His power is humble and gentle and kind. His power breathes life into fresh flowers. His power makes a way for pure love to live. He offers a way to love through the crumbing of all my imperfect statues. His love reached through time and space and all broken humanity trying to get to me. It's the same kind of love that held my face the way I held Noelle's that night under the sky sparkling with magic. When all my imperfect statues and "thou shalt nots" are broken, I can finally experience love. The kind of love that sets me free. The kind of love that whispers, "Now, go see the stars." It was the perfect day.

14

The Fourth of July

Wake up to more freedom

've waited for this exact moment the entire year!" my daughter burst out. I hope I never forget her excitement. It made everything that seemed wrong about the world right. I woke up with her words echoing inside of me. The morning after any party, the house is all out of sorts. It almost sags. The night before it carried a circus of laughter, food, and chaos, and now it needs rest and to be left alone like an introvert in recovery. The pillows are all bundled up in a corner of the couch, a nerf gun is abandoned mid-war on the coffee table, a dozen pool towels are damp and draped over the railing of the deck. The kids have happiness hangovers and zone out like zombies on screens most of the day. The fridge is jam-packed with leftovers like socks in a drawer that you can barely close. Sam's guacamole, half-eaten cheesecake bars, and grilled vegetables are all puzzled into the fridge.

I love the Fourth of July. My grandma, mom, and I were all born in July. I love it so much I named one of our daughters July. I love a home filled with bodies. I love the constant movement of people circling the appetizer table, the clamor of conversations, the kind hands that keep the drink cups filled. Clusters of friends chatting with the low beat of music in the background is what happiness sounds like to me. It's summer and the heat is on the rise. Watching people I love, love each other is perhaps my favorite cocktail. I want to drink it all. Every last drop. Waking up to a droopy home reminds me that all kinds of beauty danced here last night.

I expected celebrating the Fourth of July during Covid-19 would be depressing, like everything else with the virus had been. Everything canceled. A family reunion, a friends birthday trip, a book release party, and a kindergarten graduation for my fourth child—all canceled. Now, on the happiest of all holidays, there were no beaches, no fireworks, no large gatherings, and no front yard parades like years past. If I learned anything from Covid-19, it was how to let go and hold on at the same time. Let go of hopes, expectations, plans, dates, and deadlines, while I simultaneously held on to God and the people I loved most in this world.

That year we invited a handful of our friends, the same as in previous years, and celebrated the best we could with salsa, swimming, and the national anthem belting in the background while we watched bootlegged fireworks bounce off the night sky. Darkness covered our city, nation, and souls that year. But the kids didn't notice the changes like I felt them. They didn't notice the difference between the M-80s and the massive firework show from the year before. Instead, they squealed and pointed at the explosions flickering like light bulbs in the blackness. When my daughter screamed her heart out about waiting for this exact moment, she wasn't referring to the grand firework finale, because there was none. She didn't mean the parade or the cannonball into the deep end. She meant the magic that comes with our yearly tradition: the same people, the same cheesecake for dessert, the same sparkle in the sky, and the same summer heat. Tradition is what keeps us going when all kinds of trickiness attempt to tear us apart.

That year more than any before, I felt pulled apart. To feel put back together, I made a list of the most significant and life-changing moments in my life. I needed to feel grounded. On my list (in no particular order) were, of course, the births of my children, my wedding day, and studying abroad in Europe before my senior year of college. On the list there was the time Sam and I got tattoos in New York and ate at our favorite ramen restaurant. As I finished the list, I noticed something significant. There were certainly these unique and unforgettable moments, but more than anything, my list was marked by repeated traditions I anticipated year after year after year.

As a child, perhaps one of my favorite events was our traditional family pajama race. On Christmas Eve every year, my mom would wrap pajamas for each of us. We grabbed tight our packages wrapped in reds, greens, and twirly ribbons. Our

bodies wiggled, our hearts pounded, our voices stacked on top
of each other like a sheet cake layering up as high as possible
before toppling over with excitement. The anticipation mounting, we shouted in unison, "Three, two, one . . . GO!" We ran
down hallways, stripping down near naked, shirts flinging off,
feet tripping over pulled off jeans, and laughter erupting like it
would from lunatics in a madhouse. We slammed doors shut,
ripped open the pretty wrapping paper, yanked off tags, and
put on our new jammies as fast as a cheetah chasing prey. Yes,
this was fun, but also a race. Whoever arrived back in the family
room first won. It was a competition. A rite of passage. A trophy
to mount on your shoulders all season long.

The pajama race morphed through the years. When we got
married, more men joined the family. Instead of gifting practi-
cal pajamas, we exchanged names and made it a point to get the
most impractical ones. I'll never forget the year my brother-in-
law (a size large) ran back into the family room out of breath, face
as bright as Rudolph's nose, eyes watering, wearing a women's size
small, his pajama bottom pants up to his knees and chest hair
exploding out of his V-neck T-shirt. We laughed so hard we cried
that Christmas Eve. Now, the joke continues. Who will be the
one to get the craziest, funniest, and most ridiculous pajamas?
It's hard to beat the year someone gave my dad a skintight gold
jumpsuit. Some Christmases we have more money, while other
times there isn't much under the tree, but every year, no matter
the circumstances, we always have a pajama race.

Sam and I wanted both our families to bond more before our
first baby was born. He set up folding tables on our patio and

bought paper bowls and pumpkins. My sister Wanida had recently sent me a new recipe to try, Shelly's Chili. We were poor, but we could afford a few cans of beans. It would be perfect. I cranked open dozens of cans of Ranch Style beans, spicy Rotel canned tomatoes, and corn with anticipation of our families becoming best friends. On the Sunday before Halloween, we started the annual pumpkin carving contest. Everyone came. My in-laws are generous and good people. Sam's dad is gentle, friendly, and God fearing. His strong hug can make you feel lighter, as if his embrace absorbed all that hurt inside of you. His mom is bold. If I didn't know her well enough, I would be intimidated by her straightforwardness. But I've come to know her kindness. Sam's parents met, dated for a few weeks, and were engaged. Thirty-some years later, they were a perfect balance of soft and strong. Every year they were fierce competitors at our pumpkin-carving event. The first year no children were alive; now there are over twenty! All the kids dress up, and the older ones help the younger ones with the carving tools. Every year the rules change a little, but the constant is always Shelly's Chili and the stuffed black cat for the winner to take home until next year.

I'll never forget the year we almost canceled the pumpkin party. My boys were still babies. In early October Sam's mom called an emergency family meeting. We had just moved into "The Green House" (as we called it). Honestly, it was the most beautiful house in Old Escondido with coffered ceilings in every room, 1800s original wood floors, and a kitchen so big it could fit our entire previous granny flat inside of it. During the market crash, "The Green House" was crashing as well. While it was for sale, we were the occupants and caretakers of the property. When Sam's mom called, moving boxes still lined the hallways. Just the night before, his parents had come to see our new gem at the corner of Sixth and Hickory. I felt so proud walking them through each room. His dad especially marveled at the craftsmanship in the historic home. "Wow, wow, wow," he kept repeating with eyes wide. He promised to come over in the morning to help us set up the plumbing for our washing machine. But the phone call from his mom made us both uneasy. His mom, unshakable, was shaking. His dad, warm and full of compassion, had left the family. No one had ever left us before. No one we had ever trusted, leaned on, and called us beloved had ever walked out the door without looking back. But Sam's dad did that day. He never came over to help us hook up our appliances. In fact, he never came back again.

It seemed wrong to celebrate our traditional Halloween party. We were all a wreck and reeling. A family torn up by betrayal doesn't ever really heal. Traces of his absence are permanently left on the faces of the ones left behind. Sam has his sturdy jaw and my brother-in-law, Nate, has his brow line. It's almost as though time, events, and especially holidays break open the fleshy wound once again. It was like looking out on a wildfire. It seemed impossible to contain the potential damage. But we tried. We tried to stop the fires. But everything burned down. The flames raged higher and fiercer and angrier than we could have ever imagined. Nothing could stop the fire. We needed water dumped on us. Water to put out all the pain.

When someone you love leaves, it is as though they take all of you with them. They rip open your chest, grab your heart with their fist, and walk right out the door. It's hard to get it back. It feels impossible really. It takes a certain kind of work to get your heart back, but it's never fully the same. It can build you or break you. I saw it build some. I saw it break others. People aren't supposed to leave you. People aren't supposed to give up on a lifetime of dreams, vows, and grandbabies. People, especially the good ones, are supposed to stay forever. When someone leaves, it feels like everything leaves. All the stories, all the memories, all the security, all the hope, all the air in the room—gone.

Our families arrived the Sunday before Halloween like they always did. It was uncomfortable because we so badly wanted to be happy, but our hearts were burning. A quiet hope lived inside of me. Maybe, just maybe, our party would bring his dad back. Maybe he would love us enough to show up, beg for forgiveness, admit he was wrong, and come back home. Maybe everything would go back to normal. But he didn't knock on the door that night. We tried to sustain a strong front. The lights in the backyard still hadn't been set up, so we carved, sipped on cider, and judged each other's pumpkins by candlelight. I remember nursing my little Samuel to sleep upstairs while the family cleaned up. I remember hearing muffled laughter through the walls. It had been weeks since I had heard pure, hearty laughter. I rocked my baby and knew even in pain, gathering was good. Eating familiar chili tamed the fire inside of us all.

It was an uncertain time. A time of questioning the past and a person I thought I knew. I've wrestled with uncertainty most of my life. I didn't know how to trust myself. Everyone else knew better. Everyone else was smarter, wiser, and more well versed in life than I was. I'm not good at making decisions. I doubt and second-guess myself. When I make a choice, I worry about what people think. I can talk myself into and out of anything. I can see an argument from every side and in the end, I'm paralyzed. I have a hard time holding on to what I think. It's embarrassing. By now, I should be an adult who is self-assured and confident with my chin skyward. But I'm not. I think that's why traditions are so grounding for me. Traditions don't save me, but they pull me back to what's true.

I need truth. I think that's why week after week I've gone to church. I know I can watch it online or listen to a podcast, but I try to physically go. I wake up early, dress the kids, and twist hair into fancy fishtails. I make my way to church and sometimes sit in the service next to strangers. When the pastor invites us to meet and greet, I do it even though I'd rather crawl under my seat. I participate in the elements, wine and wafer. I partake in the weekly practice of worship, community, listening to the Word, and giving, not because I always love it, but because I need it. I need church so I can stay close to Christ. Church becomes like bumpers on a bowling lane; they keep me out of the gutter.

To be clear, church isn't a beautiful hike, a steaming hot cup of coffee, or reading a book in a hammock. Although, give me any of those things and I'd probably write my own one-hit-wonder praise song. Church isn't an Instagram photo in front of a waterfall with the hashtag #church. No, church is church.

It is a gathering with other believers in worship, confession, and listening to the spoken Word of God. It is meant to be a family. It can be a messy family, but what family isn't? Every family wraps their identity around something. For some families it's fun, sports, vacations, money, performance, adventures, or education. Some families connect by disconnecting, fighting, or simply co-existing. But the church family wraps their identity around Christ. Christ, who gives power, freedom, and love back to the family instead of consuming it all for himself. The church isn't perfect, but the intention for it is.

I went through a season where I didn't attend church. Sunday was like another Saturday. I could slowly feel my soul slip. I paid more attention to my outward appearance than to my heart. I noticed how my eyes looked at friendships, exercise, and new restaurants in order to steady the uneasiness inside of me. I began to forget my need for God. Weekly attending church doesn't save me, but it keeps me close to what I need most in this world—the meaning of why I live at all. I need constant checks in my life. I need a community of believers to confess to because my temptation, it turns out, is to always crawl under my seat. I need to sing loudly, "Tune my heart to sing thy praise," because my heart so easily goes off-key. God uses church to put all of me back into perfect pitch. So even when I'd rather sleep in—I go to

> Weekly attending church doesn't save me, but it keeps me close to what I need most in this world—the meaning of why I live at all.

church. When I would rather get a jump start on my week—I go to church. When I feel uncertain about everything in my life—I go to church. When I know my favorite worship leader is on vacation—I still go to church. It isn't perfect. But I know every Sunday, church will put me back in line with Jesus the way getting an adjustment at the chiropractor helps me stand straighter.

Every Christian has a church wound. The place that was meant to be a family may have turned against you. Perhaps it was a pastor who failed you, a doctrine that demoralized you, or a group that shunned you, but it's a wound, nonetheless. Maybe it was hypocrites who said one thing but did the other. Maybe it was that you left and no one even noticed your absence. Maybe the pastor's wife never learned your name. These wounds can still make you sick with sadness, cringe with rage, and throb with pain. Nothing hurts more than being unloved by the very thing or person that is supposed to be love. These wounds can rot your soul. They can fester like blisters always on the verge of bursting open. The sorrow is so deep it can turn you away from Christ entirely.

I see these wounds in me too. I'm tempted to turn against the church because of the wrongs that have been done to me or those I love. People I trusted gossiped about me. They pretended to like me, then spread false rumors when I left the room. Church leaders shamed those I love and never apologized. I'm tempted to throw out the whole establishment. But for as much as I have been disappointed by the church, I also have a profound love for her. It's hard to explain. I've been so furious at the things church people have said and done, but I also have such devotion, compassion, and hope for her. I've wanted space from the church, but I've never wanted to walk away entirely. When I took some time away, something in me was missing. I missed fellowship, worship, and communing with my brothers and sisters. I missed being a part of something bigger than myself. I missed God. I don't want to miss what God is doing. I don't want to miss the water because there are leaks in the well. So, I set out to forgive. Even when I'd rather wish ill on those who have done damage. Instead, I turn my chest toward them, not my back. I set my posture toward grace instead of revenge, blessings instead of bitterness, and compassion instead of combativeness.

> Oftentimes the deep work of healing takes place at the altar of pain.

We all have a church story. If yours is trapped in anger, regret, despair, or disgust, make amends. Seek restoration and redemption. The wreckage is ruining you. Oftentimes the deep work of healing takes place at the altar of pain. Through walking into our church story, we will encounter Christ. You will find the true love of Christ because He is always near the church, His people. He is always forging a way forward through humility, vulnerability, and grace. If church wounds plague you, your story isn't done yet. God will see that justice comes and full healing happens. God will make what is broken, fixed. God will see you through to the other side. You will find fullness through forgiving those who have harmed you. You will experience the sweet freedom you crave. Traditions won't be something you just do, but the lifelines that help keep your faith alive.

I can easily turn traditions into what saves me. When Sam's dad left, I was desperate to be fixed. I tried to manipulate good things into becoming *the thing* that would make all the pain stop. I tried using traditions like communion, Scriptures, and making a meal to make all my uncertainty stop. If I just did the disciplines better, my heart would feel better. But traditions aren't magic. Traditions don't heal me. Only God can do that. I so badly wanted freedom from the sadness I saw all around me, freedom from all my self-doubt and all the brokenness. I worked hard to get free of pain and free of the parts of me I didn't like. I worked to be better. But disciplines and traditions are powerless on their own.

Traditions shouldn't strangle me but set me free. Theologian Jaroslav Pelikan says it best: "Tradition is the living faith of the dead; traditionalism is the dead faith of the living."[3] Traditions ought to lead me to the One who is freedom. Traditions and spiritual disciplines, done in honesty, make a way for more freedom. The temptation will always be to find freedom by gaining more control. If I can control everything, I can get the freedom I want. If I do all the right things, in all the right ways, then my soul will be right. Traditions can become rituals done with the body, but with our hearts disengaged. Traditions are meant to ignite the heart, to wake it up like a rooster's crow. Freedom doesn't come by way of me and my control. It comes by way of Christ. Yet, my soul so easily falls asleep. That's why I need traditions. They wake me up and keep my heart activated.

I know at Halloween we will have Shelly's Chili. I know at Thanksgiving there will be my mother-in-law's dinner rolls and her homemade cranberry juice. Christmas will have the pajama race, our Christmas Eve candlelight service, and morning crepes smothered with bananas and creamy Nutella. Soon comes Easter. We marinate chicken in the secret Paschall Marinade all night long and barbecue after church. On the last day of school, we all jump in the pool with our clothes on to launch us into summer. I don't like cold water, but I do love the happy screams and bodies scrambling to get into the jacuzzi. We have "The Birthday Club." Four of my best friends from grade school and our families meet up on the first Saturday of every month to celebrate all the recent birthdays. Then on Independence Day we celebrate with cheesecake and a fireworks show. Each year, these traditions remind us of our deep need for each other and our deepest need for God.

> When I stay with my traditions, I can wake up to more freedom in Christ.

Traditions morph and change throughout the years. They've adapted and changed with age and family members. Traditions remind us of where we came from and where we are going like checkpoints on a highway. Where did you come from? Where are you going? Who are you going with? What are you leaving behind and what are you bringing with you?

Traditions allow us to stop for a moment, look at each other in the eyes, and stay awake to love.

One after the next, these markers gracefully move us forward. We anticipate the next Sunday, the first Saturday of the month, and each coming holiday. We keep looking forward with excitement because the best is still yet to come. Some traditions sting. They remind us of who we've lost, who has passed on, who is missing, or who has moved. We hold both—the joy and the sorrow. Some traditions need to be broken. Somehow being with family can bring out our old dysfunctional relational habits. We so easily slip back into our younger selves when we are with siblings. We can revert back to our familiar roles to feel safe. Traditions can be places we hide and shrink. But they can also be places where we practice growing up and out of old and unhealthy patterns. Traditions, simple and small, hook our harness onto the sturdiest cable of all, Christ. We are secure. We are strapped in. We are going somewhere. When I stay with my traditions, I can wake up to more freedom in Christ.

Wake up, sister. Feel your chest rise and fall. I know you have pain from your family of origin and your church family. I know those wounds are deep. Recall the traditions that have held you secure all these years. Those tender moments that brought you to this moment matter. Don't let traditions entangle you. Don't go through the motions of faith without engaging your heart. Every discipline starts with honesty. No tradition, no action, no discipline can do the work of salvation. They can point you to Jesus, but they can't make you a good Christian, save you, or fix you. Don't do the traditions as a way to get love, but to be connected *to* love. Where there is pain and loss, where parents and spiritual leaders have failed you, wake up to how Christ wants to bring you out of that entanglement.

Sister, wake up to the freedom story God is writing beneath the story of your traditions. Freedom can be found through the family of God. No family is perfect, but if you remain faithful, you will flourish. If you fall asleep to your spiritual longings, if your soul gets lost in the traditions of faith, if you neglect your spiritual family, your body, soul, and spirit will start to limp. Freedom is possible. Freedom awaits. Wake up to the overflowing freedom that comes from the traditions offered to you in Christ.

God gracefully calls me to buckle into the freedom that can be found through traditions. Traditions, like grace gifts, stabilize my frantic spirit. Grace gifts like church, community, tithing, and listening to Scripture. I see these grace gifts in the sparkle of my daughter's eyes as she waits for glitter to light up the sky every July. I am desperate for these gifts. I need them when life leaves me broken, beat up, and betrayed. I need them to get through the day sometimes, like coffee on a dreary afternoon. I need them to get to the top of the mountain. Through hard and impossible situations, I am attached to an unbreakable cord.

God gives us traditions to free us: drink the cup, wash the feet, love thy neighbor, dip in the water. God gives us daily markers: morning, noon, and night. God is moving the world forward in love. If we follow one marker to the next, eventually they will lead us to the top of the hill—home. A home that never droops, needs recharging, or tires of joy. The anticipation is so immense we might just burst wide open. We dream of what everything looks like from the highest peak.

One day we'll wake up and see the expansive, glorious, awe-silencing view. We won't need to know why the people we loved left us. We won't hurt about it anymore. All the uncertainty will be made certain. One day all stories will be healed. We will understand why we persevered, pressed on, and kept walking even when the fire tempted to scorch us. The grand finale is coming. It will be spectacular. It will light up the sky brighter than any firework show we've ever seen before. We won't have to fear it ever ending because it is endless. We will finally feel the freedom we've always wanted. We will see then what we can't see now. All the wrongs made right. All our heart holes, filled. All our nightmares, forgotten. All the fatherless, now in the presence of God the Father. Our eyes will be opened. Awake and fully free, we will be. Our souls will shake with unbelievable amazement like the first time holding a baby or being loved back. We will exhale. It will be so beautiful we will barely be able to breathe. But in a faint whisper we will softly sigh, "I've waited for this exact moment my entire life."

15

Palomar Hospital

Wake up to more compassion

From my bedroom window I can see a hospital. I was born there and most likely will die there. Every morning seeing the stone, cold concrete structure abruptly wakes me up. I see life and death in one blink. I put those thoughts away quickly because I have lunches to pack, bodies to dress, and last night's dishes to do. The pressure to keep up, measure up, and hurry up keeps me from letting erratic thoughts about death linger too long. But that gray building is always in my line of view. Everywhere I go, I can see it as though my mortality lives on the outside of me. This frightening thought follows me all day long: "Life is but a breath."

In the shuffle of the everyday scramble, my soul glazes over. I grab my teacup, tug open the blinds, turn on the water. I feel the temperature rise from cold to warm the way God moves time from dawn to day—slowly, but all of a sudden almost too fast. The water is hot to the touch. I say to my soul, "Wake up." And there it is, God's love. So, I open my eyes. I try not to let that foreboding building chase me like a predator. I pretend I don't see it. I go through all the motions to keep life moving forward. But I don't want to just get through life, I want to live it. I want to stay awake to this life I've been given. I want to see God right here. I want to see Him seeing me.

When someone makes prolonged, direct eye contact with me, it can be uncomfortable. It's unsettling because most people don't look square at you, like you're the only thing that matters. I twist my hair or blink another direction when someone gives me their undivided attention. I've spent much of my life wanting to disappear away into the walls. A Picasso painting hangs in my bathroom. I bought it while traveling in Spain because it captivated me. I felt like the woman in the painting was me. The woman blends entirely into the background as though her flesh is camouflage. You can only recognize her figure by the slim trace of her silhouette. She is alone and sits with her back bent over her knees. Perfectly blended hues of green, brown, and slate make this art mesmerizing. I connect to her. I am her. Sometimes I can disappear just like this woman. I can become invisible. It's a somber feeling when disappearing feels safer than standing out.

The year was piling up with loss. I felt slant. I felt lonely. Everything seemed like it was sliding and as though I was trying to walk up a downward-moving escalator. I wanted to blend into the background just like the lady hanging on my bathroom wall. It was Thanksgiving and we were hosting. When life is hard, holidays feel impossible. Even small decisions, like what time dinner is, seem overwhelming. I wasn't in a place where I could slap a happy smile on my face. I just wanted to hide. I didn't have the strength to carry conversations about things I didn't care about, suck in my post-baby stomach pouch, or worry about how loud my kids were being. I didn't have the margin to balance topics that were uncomfortable. I can't scroll past prickly topics like religion, politics, or vaccines in person like I'm prone to do on social media.

Imagine if you could scroll past people in real life, though. Wouldn't that be wild? What if as someone stood in front of you, you could touch their nose twice when you liked what they said. Tap. Tap. What if you could walk away from a conversation without any consequences when you got bored or simply lost interest in what they were saying. What if you just got up mid-sentence and left without making any excuses. I don't think we have the audacity to treat people in real life the way we treat them from behind a screen. If we took real life into screen life, we might all be a little nicer and more well behaved. We might act like adults instead of emotionally stunted teenagers. Imagine if we didn't change our tone of voice, ideology, or behavior based on where we were or who we were with. This kind of authenticity is what I was desperate for this holiday. So, on the eve of Thanksgiving, I decided I would do things differently.

We all want to be seen without making a scene.

No more blending into the background. No more controlling conversations or people. No more trying to meet everyone's expectations. This year instead of hiding myself away, I'd invite others to be with me.

I rolled out butcher paper across my dining room floor. With markers and artistry, I had one desire—be with others. One phrase kept coming to my mind as I prepared for the thirty people who would be coming over for our traditional barbecued turkey and sweet apple pie showered with cinnamon sugar. This phrase was for our family and friends, but it was mostly for me. It would be my mantra. I would repeat it when worry would creep in and fear would tempt to cripple me. Across the paper, I scribbled out these words: *You don't have to be okay to be here.* It wasn't the prettiest sign, but it conveyed the message perfectly. With Scotch tape and a stool, I stuck this sign onto my cobalt blue front door. I stepped back and smiled. This year would be less about putting on a show and more about showing people it was safe to be in my home. People don't need to wear camouflage for protection. They can come in, be themselves, and find belonging. I am trying to step out from hiding and let my voice hold space in a room too. We all want to be seen without making a scene.

Not many people have eyes to see others. We can easily see problems, tasks to complete, conflicts to resolve, and the flaws other people have. But I think some people have a special gift. The gift of sight or better yet, *in*sight. They can see inside of you. My friend Mindy is like this. She is quiet. Normally, quiet people intimidate me. I feel anxious and need to keep the conversation comfortable, bubbly, and guarded from awkward silences. But Mindy doesn't mind the silence. She makes space for it. She is taking inventory of what she sees in her surroundings. She soaks in life, beauty, and art. I can talk to Mindy about the things in my life that are meaningful to me like my children, Jesus, and the church. I can text her ad nauseam about what color to paint my bedroom, how to handle a family conflict, or how to homeschool a six-year-old. And Mindy does what she always does, she is silent. It's not because she is avoiding me. It's because she is listening. Mindy is thoughtfully preparing a Pinterest board for my bedroom paint color, crafting a prayer to pray over my family, and asking the right questions to think through a homeschooling solution.

During this particularly lonely season, Mindy would read me poetry. Every morning I'd wake up to a voice message of her reading words strung together in perfect rhythm and pace. She borrowed words from others to sustain me through another day. I'll never forget the message Mindy left for me after that Thanksgiving with the sign I taped on my door. I listened and wept. She listed all the things she saw in me. She saw my pain, my struggle, my quiet hope, and my lingering fears. She saw my courage, gifts, and love for others. She said what she saw was lovely. It was as though her words brought me to life. That woman in the Picasso painting was coming awake, gaining strength, and filling out her elegant form. I was becoming real. I was stepping into my flesh. I think that's the power of compassion. It isn't just being with someone. It is being seen by them. It is sitting with them without expectation. When Mindy was with me, I felt grounded, found, and like everything was going to be okay. Her compassion welcomed me and made space for my silence to be loud, rambling, and nonsensical. The beautiful thing about compassion is that it is a free gift to the beholder. No hooks, ties, or *you owe me something in return.*

We all need Mindys in our lives. We need people with the gift of *in*sight. People who won't rush in to resolve our issues but, instead, will sit in the tension with us. People who won't scroll past us, but stay with us. I've spent most of my life trying to understand my reality. I've so badly tried to get life right. I've tried navigating my way through this sideways world by getting more answers, being a very good person, and being seen as blameless. I've combated self-doubt and fears and stumbled aimlessly searching for the way to do everything *right.* Underneath all my toil and trepidation has been a deep longing not to be alone. I had spent so much time scrambling on the inside. I had spent so long just looking at me. *What's wrong with me— why am I so slow to figure out life? Everyone else seems fine, but me.*

When my eyes are only turned in on me, I am forced to figure out life alone. It's like the earth looking at itself and trying to determine its function. It could spin a million times and never make sense of why it's going around and around. The earth only knows its place and purpose when it is seen in the context of the sun. The earth only makes sense when it is in relationship to its life source. We will always be lonely if we are cut off from our creator. The creator of the world, sun, moon, and gigantic masses of contained water moved toward us in compassion. Christ, in compassion, lived among us. Christ, in all hope, gave us His Spirit. Christ now sits at the right hand of His Father in love. These relationships are bound by perfect unity and peace. God is the beginning, middle, and end. He is the great I AM. The chorus of all saints and angels sing, "Holy, holy, holy, is the Lord God Almighty, who was and is and is to come!" (Revelation 4:8).

As I enter into a posture of praise, I am not alone. I know another is with me when I give devotion to Christ. The veil is torn between time when my soul comes in tune with God's extraordinary, unimaginable, unfathomable existence. This God who, with a word, whispered this world into motion, moved toward me. The absurdity of this notion is beyond what I can even comprehend. I peel my eyes back from me. I bring all my angst, anger, tender hope, and fragility into this story. It all begins and ends here. I offer my heart and open my spirit skyward. I join in with the angels. My life unfolds and fills up. Here, I find the more I've been longing for. Christ is the more. Christ is hope, joy, peace, freedom, and the miracle maker. In Christ all power, safety, worth, and meaning grow. From here flows the fruit of the Spirit (Galatians 5:22–23). The closer I get to worship, the closer I get to the fullness of the life I have been looking for. My awakening happens when I enter God's story in worship and when God enters my story in love. At this intersection, I am alive.

God is always on the move to wake me up to His presence. It may be through the ding of a text, the humdrum of the daily commute, or the night sky so dark and infinite and starless echoing the coldness of my inner world; God is always tapping. He taps through disappointment and dread. He taps through my envy, lust, and gross pleasure at another's failure. God's love tap is constant, sometimes as invasive as a doorbell before sunrise or as subtle as a creek in early spring. Even in the stone-cold silence of prayer, God is present, giving me space for my truest feelings to speak. His love will never stop making its way to me. He will never stop trying to help me see the real story. No matter how tightly my eyes are closed, no matter how strung out on stress I get, or how long I hold my breath, God will keep coming. I can't escape His great compassion. He refuses to let me sleepwalk my life away.

> My awakening happens when I enter God's story in worship and when God enters my story in love. At this intersection, I am alive.

I want my eyes open. I want my heart open to His love pursuit all around me. I want to be awake to it. I want to touch it like the bleeding woman suspended in reach of Christ's garment desperate for rescue (Luke 8:44). Even in the hollow, hard, and hopeless moments of my day, "God, where are you?" When I am avoiding myself, discouraged by people's decisions, or warped in a web of anxiety, "God, how are you welcoming me into your perfect love?" While rage twists my thoughts into a tangled mess and days are saturated with sinful temptations, "God, are you with me even here?" When night moves in and my back is tired from the burdens I've picked up throughout the day, "holy, holy, holy." I am profoundly awake to the love of God with me there.

When my heart is turned to His presence with me and pursuing me, I see His gifts waiting to be received. I almost effortlessly breathe, "Thank you." I receive the beauty found in pretty shades of pink shooting up wildly like party poppers from the cherry tree outside my window. I wake up to the gift of summer wind transporting me back to my childhood days of picking dandelions and chalk-painted sidewalks and sweet licks of popsicle sugar melting down my fingertips. I enjoy the sizzle of sparkling water tickling my taste buds happy. I wake up to His love. With my palm pressed to a cool countertop, my heart cools down as well. With my eyes awake to the wonder of the blue sky intoxicating all my senses, delight and desire kiss. I present my body open and aware that every single gift I have ever been given is an extension of God's love for me. I am awake to the gifts. I am awake to the gift giver. I am living my life to the fullest because the loving presence of God is with me. No matter where I am, how I am, or what I am doing—God is present.

I know the secret to being awake. What if I told you living your life to the fullest didn't have to do with a bucket list, a beautiful body, or a bright future? What if it had nothing to do with how much you have saved in your bank account at this moment or having a family that matched your imagination or having the right kinds of friendships? What if living your best life didn't involve hustle or hurry or doing all the right habits, steps, and systems? What if being awake to your exquisite life wasn't about what you could do at all? What if being awake was as easy as opening your eyes in the morning or holding a worn-in book between your aging hands?

Here is the secret—living your life to the fullest isn't something you do on the outside. It's a beautiful, wild, risky adventure to stay awake to the loving presence of Jesus on the inside.

> When you know that you know that you know God is with you in love, you will pay attention to what matters most in our polarizing world.

God. Is. With. You. Right. Now. He is waking you up, through your circumstances, back to His compassion. This is everything. It is the gold. It is the center of gravity. When you pay attention to this, everything else finds its proper place. Here is the connection you've been craving your entire life. When you find peace here, you won't thirst for it anywhere else. You won't gulp for life from your family, career, curb appeal, or fantasy life out there somewhere. Voices will beg you, demands will startle you, dreams will tantalize you, and deadlines will pressure you, but when you know that you know that you know God is with you in love, you will pay attention to what matters most in our polarizing world.

May God help us be awake. God is the only one who can wake us from our slumber. When we are asleep, we are unconscious. We don't want to live our lives checked out, numb, or stuck. We want reality. We want to see God in the land of the living.

May God keep us awake to His loving presence and put to sleep shame that steals, anger that poisons, and pride that spoils.

May God keep us awake to His faithful work in us and put to sleep our fears, doubts, and other paralyzing thoughts.

May God keep us awake to truth and put to sleep lies that lock us up, bury, and distract us.

May God keep us awake to our desires, creativity, and wonder and put to sleep apathy, slothfulness, and boredom.

May God keep us awake to a hope-filled, good, and meaningful life and put to sleep dread, disappointment, and damaging thoughts.

May God keep us awake to the identity He has given us as children of God and put to sleep false identities that weigh us down and drag us under.

May God keep us awake to hope, peace, joy, rest, and everlasting love and put to sleep envy, greed, gossip, and other sins that slow our hearts to a bitter death.

May God, in His mercy, wake us up.

May God help us pay attention to His good presence. The God of the universe counts every single freckle and calls us "Daughter." We are intimately known and securely held in trust. We give our affection, adoration, and attention to the story of God. The stories He has written in creation, through the cross, and in our lives all coexist. With our hearts in a posture of praise, we come clean. We go from darkness to light. We open our eyes. We see the world as it truly is. We bring all of us into the truest story ever told. We abide. We are awake.

Wake up, sister. Quiet your thoughts. Allow yourself to release all of the tension your body is carrying. Can you hear your heart beating? Even as you shuffle papers and maneuver the chairs around the table, God is active. If you are separated from a spouse or anxious about everything you are lacking—God moves toward you. If you are grieving a life stage, concerned about a child, or bothered by coworkers—God always has you in His aim. If you are divorced, depleted, or dreading what you have to do tomorrow, the story beneath all these stories is how God is coming after you with gentle compassion. He wants to be closely connected to you. He promises His presence through the Word, and you get to experience it through your life.

Even when the world is pulling you apart, pay attention to what matters most—your story folding into God's story. You can see this story when you pay attention, sister. Do you see the Spirit nudging and love tapping on your life? Can you hear it? Can you taste, touch, and feel it? Even in stillness, God is moving to purge, purify, and restore your understanding of His love for you. Even when you've done nothing to deserve it, His mercies rise with the morning light to meet you. He is always waking you up. When you see how God is pursuing you in your lonely places, you will be met with compassion—a place for your silence to be loud. Offer compassion to others the way God offers it to you. Give, give, give. Be with others just as they are. Make room, open your hands, be generous with your time, resources, and expectations. Let others *not be okay*. We've received endless compassion from Christ; don't hold back from giving it. Be an agent of God's waking up grace for others. Wake up, sister. Today is all you have.

From every window on the east side of my house I see Palomar Hospital. I don't like to look at it. I don't like to think about death. It frightens me. Yet, one day I know I will die. Perhaps in the hospital where I took my first breath, I'll take my last.

Life is a moment. As I watch my mother age, my father lose his strength, and my son's eyes look down at me, I know this to be true. While I have life, I desperately want to live it. I lay aside the idea of running after life. Instead, I receive it. I want to soak it in the way Mindy does with me. I just get to listen. I want to receive life the way she recited poetry to me with grace. How I live rests entirely on who lives within me.

One day, sooner or later, this reality will end, and a new one will begin. My body will stop being. When I arrive at that moment, I want to know that I didn't spend days, weeks, months, years, or even seconds of my life needlessly trying to appease my God who loved me even before I took a breath. I want to know that I didn't wrestle, toil, and fear my standing before Him. I want to know that I trusted His divine presence in my life. I hope I believed that God was always growing me into the best, most beautiful version of me.

When my life comes to a slow halt, I want to know I didn't beg, control, or spend precious time agonizing over people's approval of me. I want to know I didn't spend my whole life awake to things that didn't matter, trying to get people to like me, living for someday, or juggling a to-do list just to feel important. I want to know that I walked slowly through the winter storm and felt the cold rush of rain on my skin. I want to know I stood outside long enough to feel the wind tangle my hair and chased after the buttery golden light with gravel under my bare feet. I want to know that I looked my children in the eyes and let them dream impossible dreams. I want to know I stood on the edge of my inner abyss with Jesus and didn't shy away. I want to know I talked to the stranger and held open my home for the hopeless. I want to know I had long, meaningful, honest conversations with people I loved. I want to know I didn't grab after life like a desperate creature but savored mindless tasks like holding hands with my husband, tinkering on the piano, or slicing plump tomatoes from our garden. I want my arms filled with an absurd amount of lilac stems bursting my heart wide in praise. I want to stay up way too late on Monday nights and eat breakfast for dinner multiple times a week. I want to watch still water. I want to extravagantly love people with gifts they don't deserve or even thank me for. I want to always keep learning, cheer loud for the underdog, and help my parents grow old. I want to know that I lived freely because I was, in fact, free.

I hope I was always awake to the simple yet profound glory of God's saving grace in my life. And even if I wasn't, even if I fail and never do any of these incredibly lovely things, I think that's okay too. I believe God will love me with unwavering adoration if I fail or succeed, always struggle to trust Him, and succumb to the same exact sins my entire life. His awake-ness toward me was never earned by my merit, capacity, or competency. It was always just because He wanted to be with me. As wild as it is to imagine, to Him, my life was worth His death.

Sister, you don't have to worry or calculate anymore. You don't have to stress out about living life to the fullest. You don't have to figure out how to be a human, you just get to be one. It's almost too easy. You get to have an adventure of a lifetime, even if you never own a passport. Perhaps this is what Jesus meant when He said, "My yoke is easy, and my burden is light"

(Matthew 11:30). If following Jesus is a heavy load, you aren't following Jesus. Your path will have challenges, but the way is made possible because He promises to never leave us alone. Don't wait for a nightmare to wake you up. Don't wait for a loved one to believe or the church to get it right. Don't wait. Don't wait. Tap your chest, turn your affection to the light, and keep this prayer close to your lips: "God, keep my heart awake to your love." Let your awake-ness be your worship. This life is a breath, sisters. I intend to live mine deeply, faithfully, and with clunky courage. No more chasing after life. Instead, I'm connecting to it. I am receiving it. Deep breath in. Deep breath out.

When the day of my death comes, my soul won't pause. Not even for a second. It won't even blink, hesitate, or stall. My soul will always be entirely awake. This life is not the end. With gentleness and warmth, I will be welcomed. I might be afraid, but I'll also have an unexplainable peace. I will know the sound, taste, touch, sight, and aroma of the One waiting for me. They will be as familiar as the orange trees circling my childhood home. Anticipation will be sparked as when hearing a Christmas hymn when the season first begins. I'll be coming home to the home I've always felt, but never fully known or experienced. Grace will usher me in the way Mindy did and God always does. I won't be alone. The same sign hangs then, now, and forever. It isn't taped or written on butcher paper but held with wounded hands and written across a resurrected body. God made a way for His goodness to meet my humanness. God's heart pulses and expands with compassion. I'll have nothing to offer but me. The sign will be like mine at Thanksgiving, yet far more compelling. I'll want to run forward. A new adventure within arm's reach. God welcomes me with *living* words: "You don't have to be okay to be here." I close my eyes and open them. "Holy, holy, holy." I will be fully awake.

Discussion Questions

Thoughts to consider

── **Introduction: The Whole Truth** ──────────

1. Name what you are most awake to in your life right now. What concerns, relationships, fears, or dreams occupy most of your time and mental space?

2. How would you describe your heart in this season: asleep, sleepwalking, or fully awake?

3. Share the times in your life when you were most awake.

4. What is the story beneath your story right now? (Take a moment to think about something you are struggling with. Now consider how God is awakening you into more intimacy, knowledge, or trust through that circumstance.)

Chapter One: My Name

1. Can you share a time when your life felt meaningless?
2. Describe a moment when God's love met you in your greatest pain.
3. If you could imagine God's new name for you, what would it be?

   (The one whom God _____.)
4. What meaning is God awakening in your life right now?

Chapter Two: RSVP

1. What are some of the tests (good and bad) you use to determine if someone is worthy of your trust?
2. Do you have a hard time believing people like you?
3. Is it hard for you to show up and be fully yourself? Explain.
4. Do you believe God fully accepts you?

Chapter Three: The Luckiest

1. If you created a soundtrack for your life, what songs would be on it and why?
2. Where have you been fishing for worth where worth can't be found?
3. Has a person or experience diminished your sense of worth?

4. If you could imagine God singing an "I love you more than" song over you in your current season of life, what would it be?

Chapter Four: A Knock at the Door

1. Who comes to mind when you think of someone humble? What evidence of humility do you see in their life?

2. What spiritual issues are still challenging for you to understand?

3. What metaphor comes to mind when you think about your spiritual journey?

4. Is there a situation in your life where you need wisdom?

Chapter Five: There Was an Accident

1. Describe the life transitions you are in right now.

2. What do you need to grieve?

3. How can you make space for hope to grow?

4. Share about someone in your life who has passed away.

Chapter Six: Thin Spaces

1. Share a meaningful "thin space" in your life.

2. Describe a miracle that God has done for you.

3. What are you most grateful for right now?

4. Who is God inviting you to share the miracles He has done in your life with?

—— **Chapter Seven: Water** ————————————

1. Is it easier for you to feel anger or sadness? Why?

2. Write a list of childlike requests.

3. Do you tend to express your feelings or suppress them?

4. Is there a discipline you can put into practice that involves water? (running water over your feet for a few minutes a day, drinking more water, swimming)

—— **Chapter Eight: Glass-like Glory** ————————

1. Do you remember how you felt or what you did when there was conflict in your home as a child?

2. Name people in your life you can give back to God.

3. Where do you feel fragile right now?

4. Does God feel safe to you? If not, explain how He has been unsafe.

5. Describe a few ways God is waking you up to His safety.

—— **Chapter Nine: Dish Towel** ————————————

1. Name a person in your life who has remained faithful.

2. Name a few things or people God has asked you to be faithful to right now. Be honest about how you feel about those people or tasks.

3. Who can you pick up a towel for today?

4. If you are in a season of suffering, how do you experience Christ waking you up to His presence?

Chapter Ten: The Monster Is Coming

1. Make a list of your monsters. What are you most afraid of?

2. How do you respond to conflict? Do you move toward it, run from it, or pretend it isn't there?

3. Do you experience God's presence in your biggest fears?

4. Take a moment to imagine Jesus awake to you in your worst-case scenario. Describe what that is like.

Chapter Eleven: This Is Not the End

1. What evil pain can you identify in your life (events that still feel attached to shame)?

2. Name the agreements you have made.

3. How are you awake to the reality of spiritual warfare in your life?

4. Spend some time speaking authority over these agreements.

Chapter Twelve: Debbie from the Plane

1. Where is God inviting you to more sacrifice in your life?

2. In what ways are you experiencing joy in your day-to-day life?

3. Describe a detour in your life that God used for good.

4. How is God waking you up to His love in your story?

—— **Chapter Thirteen: It Was the Perfect Day** ——

1. What are your "thou shalt nots"?
2. Describe the idols that you have propped up on a shelf.
3. What idols is God, in His grace, breaking in your life right now?
4. How are you waking up to more of God's power in your life?

—— **Chapter Fourteen: The Fourth of July** ——

1. Consider the traditions you were raised with.
2. Has anyone you've ever trusted left you?
3. What did your family of origin wrap their identity around?
4. Share wounds that you have experienced in the church.
5. In your experience, do traditions enslave you or set you free?

—— **Chapter Fifteen: Palomar Hospital** ——

1. What do you fill your loneliness with?
2. Which friend offers you compassion? Explain.
3. How is God love tapping on your life right now?
4. Are you awake to the story of God's love for you?

Acknowledgments

Dad, thank you for faithfully praying.

Mom, thank you for teaching me what it means to be awake.

Leonie, thank you for being a safe sounding board.

Malina, thank you for making everything more fun.

Wanida, thank you for being a compass pointing me back to Christ.

Krissa, thank you for your edits, voxes, and forever friendship.

Kara, thank you for challenging me to dream bigger.

Becca, thank you for meeting me at the ocean.

Mindy, thank you for your compassion and poetry.

Ashley, thank you for daily grace and for saying yes to adventures.

Kristin, thank you for your support and for all the beautiful flowers.

January, thank you for making me laugh and being a faithful friend.

Katie, thank you for your honesty and vulnerability.

Jessica, thank you for your thoughtfulness.

Aly, thank you for your authenticity.

Melissa, thank you for your prayers.

Erin, thank you for your magnetic joy and love for Jesus.

Amanda, thank you for our camping trip conversations.

Brenda, thank you for your willingness to always help.

To my nieces and nephews: Naomi, Aria, Juliet, Eleanor, Matthew, Hezy, Lelina, baby girl Botica, Jackson, Ethan, Zoey, Claire, Gwen, and Colton. I love being your auntie! I pray you live lives fully awake to the love of God.

To all the teenagers, children, and babies that come through our front door—you are always welcome here! Eat all the food in the pantry, jump in the pool, and if you need someone to listen, you can find me by the fire pit. If you ever need a place to call home, you have one here.

Greta, thank you for your stories, faith, and all kinds of other silliness.

Becky, thank you for your lists and dinner ideas, and for really praying.

Rissa, thank you for always speaking truth with a splash of humor.

Jenn, thank you for picking up where we left off.

Manda, thank you for always cheering me on.

Colleen, thank you for sticking with me.

Rachel, clear eyes, full hearts, can't lose.

Jesse, I'm just so grateful for you.

Mission Hills Church and staff, thank you for being family.

IG community, thank you for letting me be vulnerable and loving me back.

Some Day is Here community and staff, thank you for teaching me so much.

(in)courage sisters, thank you for carrying my burdens and writing such important stories.

Thank you to those who helped me with the cover of this book: Jacob, Sarah, Leonie, Maria, Ashley, Wanida, and Miles. And, of course, thank you to Shantalice, the rooster. You were radiant.

Bethany House team, thank you for your guidance and believing in me.

Jennifer Dukes Lee, thank you for shaping my stories with your wisdom, kindness, and encouragement. You are a gift.

Lisa Jackson, thank you for being my advocate.

To those who let me share their stories, thank you.

Children, my prayer is that you will always know the loving presence of Jesus. Thank you for giving me "just five minutes" to write when I needed it.

Manoah, your passion is incredible to witness.

Samuel, your deep soul is a gift to know.

Noelle, your courage teaches me.

Hannaly, your light is contagious.

Mea, your life is pure delight.

Sam, thank you for always being awake to me.

Notes

1. U2, "40," Tempe, AZ, 1987, www.youtube.com/watch?v=lj8rz XBVmBY.

2. Thomas Merton, *Thoughts in Solitude* (New York: FSG, 1958), 83.

3. Joseph Carey, "Christianity as an Enfolding Circle [Conversation with Jaroslav Pelikan]," U.S. News & World Report, 106 (25), June 26, 1989, 57.

About the Author

Anjuli Paschall grew up encircled by an orange grove in San Diego. After graduating from Point Loma Nazarene University, she earned her master's degree in spiritual formation and soul care from Talbot Seminary. She currently lives in Southern California with her husband, Sam (a pastor), and their five children. Anjuli writes regularly for (in)courage and offers online courses and spiritual direction. Her writing has been featured in *Christianity Today*, Pop Sugar, and Her View From Home. She loves chai tea, golden hour, the ocean, and the color orange.

Instagram: @lovealways.anjuli

www.anjulipaschall.com

More from
Anjuli Paschall

We search for a connection with God but can't seem to escape the haunting feelings of guilt, shame, loneliness, and fear. Through raw stories, Anjuli Paschall invites you to stop running from your pain and to recognize that the deep end of your story is the way to intimacy with Christ. It's time to reach inward and heed the quiet voice whispering, *Stay.*

Stay